EARTH HEALING

Happy Publishing

Foreword

Anushree Agarwal

A few years back, I had a vivid dream. In the dream, I was talking to Mother Earth; I saw how the whole earth is also designed by the Universe just like we as humans are. How as a Being, it has taken upon itself to nurture and support the life on the planet and support the vibrational shift of life in the Universe. How just like us- the humans, the earth also has multiple energetic layers and how we as humans co-create and contribute to the vibrational frequency of the planet.

How we anchor the emotional layer of the planet with our thoughts, feelings, emotions.

How we anchor the mental layer of the planet with our beliefs, structures and attitude.

How we shift the reality and vibration on the planet with our intent, awareness, and ability to contribute.

And how, Earth with the energy of Creation and different laws sustains our living, ascension and evolution.

It was a dream. And the beginning of something new in paradigms of awareness and evolution in my life.

I started becoming more aware of how a space is more conducive to one's growth where there are more trees, flowers which in turn attract more birds, bees, insects and other forms of living. I started noticing how any space which had all the kingdoms - crystalline, plant, bird, animal, humans in balance and harmony could create a sense of joy and bliss and how people including myself would naturally be more enthusiastic and active to Be and do more with every moment of living.

On the contrary, I also noticed, places where there was an absence of plants, or birds or animals and places were also the places where humans were more stressed, unhappy and cribbing.

I started noticing the houses and setups where humans were more grateful for life, and kind to each other and contributing to earth with their awareness of what can make the soil more fertile, feeding the birds, animals, treating animals with respect were also the communities where there was more joy, good health, the energy of prosperity, the sense of belonging ness and a sense of bliss. Kindness was a natural by product and pleasantness exuded everywhere.

One may wonder how is this all connected to Earth healing. And it's valid too. As an earth healer, and after clearing the Earth portals across the world in some key locations, one key understanding I have had in my meditations is that everything on this planet has been our creation. The density or choked feeling in a place is directly proportional to the number of massacres, trauma and the pain that the collective has experienced in that location. Each action of us, each thought creates a vibration that in turn affects the overall well-being of all the kingdoms on that location.

Hence it is very important, that with the shift in consciousness we are currently undergoing on the planet, we acknowledge our roles in creation of a beautiful planet and we take the right steps both physically in terms of concrete actions, mentally and emotionally in terms of our attitude towards the planet and translate that into a living reality both for us and future generations.

It's important that we put our energies in the spaces that creates a vibrational shift and expansion for every living species on the planet.

I truly wonder how much more beauty this planet will exude for generations to come as we put our hearts together and seep in the roots of harmony and bliss.

I hope this book opens up those tiny little windows in each of us and allows our pleasantness to shine through every door.

Table of Contents

CHAPTER 1

The Stone Reader

Christine Caruso

"They didn't."

A woman once asked why the Stones had chosen me.

"They didn't," I told her.

"They choose everyone.

Everyone.

But not everyone chooses them back."

I, quite simply, did.

I happen to talk to rocks. Or more accurately, I listen to them. They do most of the talking.

All of Nature seeks a relationship with us. Literally. And it is one of the sweetest, purest relationships to cultivate. But it's a relationship that requires us to not judge ourselves, and sustaining that can be a bit of a bugger sometimes. Especially in this crazy interesting world.

I grew up in a little town called Queens, New York. In a noisy house of wild Italian-Irish people squished together. Oh, the yelling from room to room. The talking over each other. And that was when we *weren't* fighting. The non-stop and ever-pressing sounds of the endless news programs and the radio. This was not exactly a zone of tranquility.

So, when our parents seated all four of us girls in the back of the Crown Victoria and ushered us to a dairy farm in Pennsylvania, I thought I had reached Heaven.

Silence. Silos. Grass. Animals. And what was that thing I was feeling inside myself... that thing as I ran around hills and smelled manure and hay... what *was* that? I wasn't certain, but my body demanded more.

I didn't know it at the time, but I had fallen in love with the bare earth. Around her, I felt so alive. This little 5'2 chicky finally felt massive and heard. Mother Earth was listening, so I kept talking. I would find anywhere and everywhere to be alone in nature. I always had this feeling that She not only understood me, but knew me, deep in my bones.

And so, this began my first long-lasting relationship of no-judgment. Of trust. Of pure, inconceivable expansion and clarity, like the ringing of the bell of water as she falls from a high peak.

And my desire to experience that crystal clarity of Earth has brought me all over the planet, and into a deep space of connection with some of the oldest creatures of the Earth: The Stones.

When I was in my early 20s and living in the heart of Washington, DC, I finally put these glorious Stones into a fishbowl. Over the years I had collected them, and God they looked so beautiful when they were in water. Why not keep them in this perfect glass bowl, and stare at them? It sounded to me like a perfectly natural thing to do. My roommates, utterly baffled (one an attorney and the other a teacher) looked at me like I was a rather unusual species (I also introduced them to the joy of candles and baths, for that matter. This is how I roll).

Silent whispers and nudges in my awareness would tell me what to do with the Stones. And years later, when working in a wellness center as an Energy Healer, I began to use them. Throw them. Place them. Listen to them. When you finally get over yourself, (yes there were plenty of times I doubted what I was doing) and do it, the Stones start to give you more and more, like an anxious new best friend.

"Oh, you're listening? Here. Have this... and this... and this..."

They tell me of diseases, of messages from loved ones past as well as alive. They take the shape of people's spines and bones and show me someone's child's capacities. They are active and engage dynamically with the energy present.

Each time we throw them, the dynamic changes. Because they are the oldest creatures on the planet, they seem to hold and share the wisdom and sight with pure generosity of spirit and possibility. They are both fierce, and beautiful.

They roll off tables and pop into people's laps. There are no coincidences which ones fall repeatedly when I try to gather them into my hands. They are so alive, playful, powerful, serious, colorful. In one moment a shade will darken or a new line will suddenly become visible in a stone.

The lines they fall into, the shapes they take... there is no pattern. They are the unbridled energy of pure creation. And if my mind could get out of the way, they might finally dance in the air.

As time passed, I began to hear an unusual language as well. Afraid to appear as a bit of a strange bird, I kept it to myself, until finally it became like a dam preparing to break in me. The energy it takes to *not* be ourselves is overwhelming. It can be rather exhausting to hold ourselves back from who we truly be.

Finally, I just couldn't hold it in anymore. And when I began to speak it, and honor what I was hearing, HOW THINGS CHANGED. Dramatically. And Fast.

During sessions, I would hear the sounds clearly and speak them, aware of the energy they contained and how it was directly connecting through and communicating with the person. After time, I began to speak the sounds I heard, then speak English. Speak the sounds. Speak English. A client finally pointed out: "You know, you are translating for me."

I hadn't even noticed. I was so given over to the energy and the experience,

Listening.

At the time, for some reason I could never find any information on the internet about what I was doing. Curiously, I never found a name for the practice. For years. And how prospective clients would look at me like a wild child and ask: "You mean, you don't read tarot? Or Angel Cards? What about my palm? Can you at least read my palm?"

I would rarely respond to their questions, and just shrug my shoulders in silence. Either they knew this was for them, or not. If they couldn't hear their knowing telling them yes or no, they certainly wouldn't hear the Stones.

So, on we went. My great companions and me. Over time, the Stones developed archetypes and names. New ones were added to the pouch, either from the Earth or from individuals. The collection grew and so did our relationship.

The Black Madonna was a gift from a man who had returned from Iceland. He did not know I was a Stone Reader. We had met briefly at a Buddhist retreat we were both attending. At the closing dinner, he was inspired to offer me the choice of one sweet black smooth Stone, typical of the region from his travels.

"The Stones there are known for the faces in them. It is believed you look into them and see a thousand faces." He had been given five to bring back to the States. Quite simply, he wanted to give me one.

I looked at him, no longer surprised (yet always in awe) by how new Stones found their way into my pouch. So, I selected Her, brought her to the pouch, and set her among friends.

It takes time before their names and ways become apparent to me. They challenge me and teach me to be patient. Some Stones spend quite some time as Place Holders on the mat, before they move into the collective to be thrown.

> *"But can you listen?*
>
> *Without saying a word?"*

She became the Black Madonna. Fierce. Cutting through Fears, and Shadows. If there were aspects of oneself that we were afraid of, or rejected, she brought them into the Light. She was the fiercest one in the pile. When She started speaking, it was not a "Go Gently into the Night" type of session.

Not one single bit.

For years She worked so hard, and one day when I opened the pouch, she was gone. Gone. I knew She had done her time, and was complete with us. They disappear like that sometimes. I don't ask questions. I have learned, it is an honor to have them for as long as they stay, and then when they are complete, they move on.

Trust.

It's about letting go of what I think, and what I *think* I think, and what is Right and what is Wrong. What is Appropriate, and what is Precious. These things are thoroughly and utterly different to all. Being willing to Let Go, especially when you are asked to, has been the most unusual journey.

Many years ago, I was at a festival in Asheville, NC doing a Stone Session for a mother and her son. And I received direction to give the young boy a particular stone of mine. I battled this for a few moments, silently. I did *not* give Stones away. These were here for a particular reason. These were not just whimsical little things to pass along.

But I heard it again, and again. Insistent. This had nothing to do with me, and I had to get over myself and what I thought I was supposed to be doing. So, I let go. I explained to the mother about the gift of the Stone, as her son was young to understand certain aspects. But the gift was clearly for him, and he would know what to do with it, in his most beautiful purest way.

I watched them walk away with one of the Stones. Letting Go.

About an hour later, a different young boy came to me.

So shy and quiet, he reached out his hand to me: "I just wanted to give this to you."

In his hand was a Stone.

He didn't know the other boy. He hadn't seen our exchange earlier.

He just knew. And listened. And did what he knew.

Trust.

One great day, I met a woman who traveled often to Peru, studying for years with the Shamans there. She saw us working, and incredulous at what she was witnessing, asked me where I learned this.

"I didn't," I told her. "I just do it."

"You just do it? This is a 10,000-year-old tradition from the Q'ero people in the highlands of Peru."

And just like that, they let me know.

I write this chapter from one of the islands in the Caribbean that was destroyed by a hurricane so massive, they could not categorize it. I survived it, and the aftermath, with 3 friends in a closet. Because much of the infrastructure here was stronger than some of the other islands affected, only about 90 percent of St Marten was ravaged. Whereas, islands such as Dominica and Barbuda have become almost obsolete.

About three weeks before Hurricane Irma came along, I received this channel. For some reason, I never sent it out to my email list or onto FB as originally guided to. It is curious how now, it applies even more:

"We [the Stones] are to be cherished.

To remind you of this pure energy of communion, of TRUST.

Of the trust in Yourself that told you to believe in Us.

You believed when your mind suggested you shouldn't.

Now help Us remind everyone else.

You can't not be awake anymore. Not because the Earth is suffering. Or nature dying.

The Earth will exist after You. She will. Her surface may look different, but She knows how to rejuvenate.

No, it's not for the Earth.

It's for You.

You must wake up.

The only reason Trees die, Waters dry up and Air becomes a stagnation of pollution, is to show you to WAKE UP.

Parts of Us may die, but Earth will always come back.

All of you will die, and you will not come back.

Wake Up.

Life is Beautiful.

It took Us millions of years to form. It will take Us many more to deconstruct. You, my little ones, do not have that luxury.

Wake up, Little Ones.

Wake up.

Or you will be asleep forever."

Five days and two Hurricanes later, we were evacuated. Jose, the second hurricane, never ended up hitting us. Miraculously, in one day he went from a Level 4 (certain death for us after surviving a Level 5 plus) to a Level 2, and then decided to leave us alone entirely.

I never even saw the rain that night.

We were allowed to bring very little as we ran to the helicopter evacuating us to St Kitts. My pouch of Stones never left my side. A bit of a weight to carry when you must run past a military blockade to get to your destined evacuation, but we tore on.

Three weeks ago, I returned to St Marten, to "help" her rebuild. But I think it was really to find these pieces of my heart that fell out when Irma came. I carry my pouch of Stones to different spaces on the island and Listen. I pick up my Heart-Pieces.

And realize, now more than ever, as I was told months ago in the channel,

She's not asking me to heal Her.

Not one single bit.

She's asking me to heal me.

Christine Caruso
St. Maarten, French West Indies

The Author

Christine Caruso
www.HealingEarthBook.com/christine-caruso

CHAPTER 2

The Ridge

Ben Noble

She was everything to me and I knew she couldn't be.

I was receiving a healing session from a dear friend when the vision of the Ridge came. "Come to me and sing your song," it said—the call was unmistakable. I saw myself in the golden desert, standing on a ridge and singing to the sky. I knew the place the moment I saw it in my mind's eye. As I sat there with my friend, pondering the vision, I let the plans I had for my weekend crumble as a new path took their place. I went home and contacted the lodge near the ridge to make a reservation, tossed some things for the trip in my car and set out for the eastern Oregon desert.

I had been there once a year before. Waking up that morning next to Holly I felt this powerful pull to go east and be in the rocks and sand. She knew of a place and together we created a beautiful day of magic and presence. Hiking in the beautiful desert, making love atop the ridge with the warm winds caressing our bodies, surrendering to each other in the fullness of our love and adoration... So much had changed since then.

Now I was journeying alone. The pungent desert juniper filled my nostrils as the forest that surrounded Mt. Hood fell away and I passed into the open desert. Something about that smell and hot air soothed my body, like home. I was welcome here.

There always seemed to be a woman in my life I realized as I checked into my room at the lodge, enjoying the strangeness of being solo. Over the last 10 years I had been married twice and divorced twice. While many of the people my age were partying, and finding their way in the world I was going to church and getting married. Always on a perpetual quest to purify myself and get "right" with God. The addiction to porn killed my first marriage. The buried wounds of my childhood abuse killed my second. And diapers, so many diapers... when this stay-at-home dad got to three kids in diapers at once there was a breaking point. I had to go.

And then there was Holly. I didn't last more than a month without some kind of relationship before I fell head over heels for her. Sitting across from her in the hot tub at our friend's party, she was being fawned over by some guy and I had my arms around some girl. As she stood to grab her drink from the side of the hot tub, reaching across I saw the full stretch of her body and those beautiful brown thighs, oh those thighs... In that moment I knew I was a gonner.

Stepping out onto the balcony of my room with the smell of baked grasses and juniper lifting my body to the edge of everything, I set my mind to what lay ahead. So many wonderful experiences and so many mistakes had led me to this point and, yet I knew that after my date with the ridge tomorrow morning, everything was going to be different. I had a light dinner then spent some time in the pool and hot tub always looking for the possibility of a pretty face coming around the corner to catch her eye and smile, but none came. Looks like I'll be spending the night alone I thought as I spread across the width of the king-sized bed in my room and settled in to sleep.

The next morning, I woke early. Stepping onto the balcony I drew a deep breath of the desert air so warm and nurturing to my naked body. Scents of juniper and wild grasses lingering from the cooler night, not yet baked by the blazing day. My soul was at ease, receiving the gift of the golden hills and plateaus that filled my view, still tainted with the rose of dawn.

Today I was just me.

I ate way too much for breakfast. They had a buffet and I piled the food on my plates like there was never going to be another egg broken in my life again. I didn't know how to prepare for a journey like this. All I knew is I was hiking up to a hot desert ridge alone and I wasn't coming back until whatever needed to happen, happened. I texted Holly and another female friend to let them know I was doing this for real. I'm not sure what I was hoping for in their response like the yearning for my mother's approval when I finished building a Lego starship. But enough of that now. It's time to go.

Sandals, shorts and tank-top on (the exact same outfit I wore when I was here last) water, my phone (turned off), "Dad Off-Duty" ball cap my ex-wife had given me as a joke for Father's Day last year, and the elk-tooth medicine wheel necklace Holly's birth mom had gifted me for Christmas, I was ready.

As I started the ascent to the top of the first big hill I was surprised how quickly I was gasping for air, I gotta get out more. Resisting the urge to drink I kept pushing my body onward to the top of the first rise. I could see the beautiful golden hills all around and the river below the lodge, cutting its way through the valley dividing it in half. Above me rose the wizened cliff faces of the main ridge, majestic, deep shadows thrusting their features into the sun. Hiking a little further I came to a T where the path split. To my left was the route Holly and I had followed around one side of the main ridge to the top and to the right was another path that cut between the main ridge and another slightly smaller ridge to the east. I chose to go right.

Within moments my choice was met with a heart-stopping screech as the tall grass field to my left exploded in a flurry of motion. I froze and then laughed at myself as I saw the pair of desert grouse lift into the sky together.

The first omen came as I wound my way up the dusty trail, my mouth sticking from the thirst, a single hawk feather drifted from the sky and fell at my feet. Well that's got to be a good thing to receive on your first soul journey into nature, I thought! I must be on the right track here. I picked up the feather and slid it behind my ear as I marched on, lifted.

God, it was good to be out here! To be alone and yet part of everything; the sage bushes and wild grasses, the rocks and dirt, the wild creatures, the warm dry air bringing all the smells and sounds to me, and the few gnarled juniper trees dotting the trail that seemed to show up every time I desired a moment to sit and rest.

As I got closer to the top the two ridges loomed before me. I knew the trail would curve in between and around the back of the main ridge leading to the place on the edge where Holly and I had joined our bodies together on that perfect day... She was always the planner, packing blankets, pillows, food, headlamps and juice boxes for every trip- even to the movie theater! That day though, that day she trusted me, that day she let me lead. That day we followed the magic of what was possible when you just go and trust that everything you need will show up. That day we gathered a few snacks at our favorite neighborhood grocery store, put them in the cooler and set off. I'll never forget the first time I smelled the western juniper as we left the evergreen skirt of the mountain and entered the open, high desert. It was different than anything I had smelled before. It was like an acrid pine mixed with cat urine and sunny warmth. It filled the whole landscape with its presence. It was like a color, a smell, a flavor, a feeling all at once.

I remember noticing the smaller ridge when I was there a year before. I remember it being the first of the two ridges that I was drawn to. It wasn't as big as the main one but jutted out more dramatically, the open space of the valley surrounding it on all sides. When Holly and I had done our first hike to the larger ridge I was disappointed to discover that there were no trails leading over to the smaller ridge. Yet as I climbed upward this day it kept pulling my attention. When I found myself nestled between the two ridges it seemed I had a choice: follow the trail up and to my left to the familiar ridge where I had made love to my beloved or forge a new path? Dropping my senses deep into my body I was aware of an opening, a spaciousness, a lightness to my right; inviting me and my body to spill over into the new possibilities that were waiting there.

My feet crunched the blackened wild grasses littered over the stones and sand, there had been a fire here, probably started by lightning. As I neared the top of the ridge there was a patch of sand where the grasses had burnt away to the edges creating a circle. In the center of the circle there was a small red rock. I reached down to pick it up between my fingers and as I lifted discovered that it was actually a larger red rock buried under the scorched earth. Holding it in my hand I noticed it looked like a human heart, I squeezed and felt the pulse of my fingers against its hard-smooth surface. At the edge of the circle I noticed a gnarled piece of wood woven in the sand. I curled my fingers around the dry wood and lifted it out of the earth. In my hand I held a twisted staff that perfectly fit my grip, the charcoal from its burnt edges blackening my fingers. I wondered if I held in my hands the relics of some sacred ceremony from ages past. They were a part of my journey now. Staff in my right hand, heart in my left, and feather anointing my crown, I mounted the Ridge.

After crossing over the lip of the Ridge and onto the plateau something was different. I was aware of the presence of ceremony, of ritual, of the sacred. Seeing the glint of the sun in the golden hairs on my tanned arm as the stifling breeze brushed them back and forth, smelling my sweat fused with the scent from the nearest of the four juniper trees spaced along the edge of the ridge overlooking the valley, with the bold blue sky overhead challenging the amber landscape below to look up and behold. Reverently, I removed my clothes and sandals leaving them in a neat pile next to my back-pack. Wearing only my elk-tooth necklace and hawk feather, with heart and staff in hand, face and body anointed with charcoal symbols, I stepped through the portal and into the otherworld.

Moving slowly at first, feet still adjusting to all the sharp rocks and prickly grasses, I scanned along the edge of the Ridge for the place that I would sing my song. That's when I spotted the glint of gold peeking out from a rupture in the side of the cliff. As I approached the enchanted glow my body filled with the energy of possibility. Standing over the golden bowl I fell to my knees, plunging my fingers into the earth feeling the dirt fill every crevice of my dry hands. Digging my nails deeper I felt my palm graze against something solid. I brought my hands together and lifted them up, crumbling chunks sifting through my fingers as they rose, slowly revealing the hidden treasure. I stared blankly at a handful of large gold coins. As I began to grasp the abundance and wealth the planet is so willing to gift to us I laughed, and my vision opened to see a cascade of gold erupting from the side of the ridge beneath me and showering the valley below with its ever-giving richness. I scooped my hands into the golden flow over and over again washing my hair, head and body with it until my body was saturated in golden light. You never know who or what you might encounter on a journey of the soul, so I kept two of the gold coins for whatever might lie ahead and continued on.

When my feet stopped I knew I had reached the place of singing. Every choice had led up to this moment, this place. Who was I now and who would I be after? Fear of loss was not an option anymore for everything I thought I valued was already gone, fallen away, leaving just me and nature.

I stood forth on the edge of the Ridge. Drawing the energy of the earth up through my feet settled in the dry dirt, up through my legs, my cock, my abdomen, filling my arms and hands, swelling in my chest. Inhaling a breath to the bottom of my spine and exhaling I rocketed my song through my dry throat into the devouring hot wind. I sang until the breath was gone then digging deep, I sang again. The sound was not pretty. Every wretch and croak tearing from my body sounded as if a dozen of the ragged desert hawks scanning overhead had been gathered in a canvas bag and then beaten against the cliff wall until they were nothing but blood, bone, and feathers.

And I sang. I sang to the sky. I sang to the neighboring ridges. I sang to the valley below. I sang with all my heart, soul, power and vulnerability. I sang to all my lost loves. I sang to my children. I sang to the hidden fears of the shy boy trying to make himself invisible in the corner. I sang to the bitterness of a lost marriage and dream. I sang to the grief of losing the father I longed to be... And I sang to the future. I sang to the hope of a life reborn. I sang to the souls I came here to bless and the light I came to shine. I sang to the joy of passing through the shadows and discovering the greatness on the other side.

And the song was perfect.

I stood proudly, sun on my naked skin, twisted stick in my hand, feet gripping the earth, arms stretched to the east and west encompassing all, knowing I had accomplished my invitation.

"Come, and sit under my branches..." she called. I turned to see the third of the four juniper trees directly behind me. As I approached I saw that some of her branches were blackened and burned, she must have been struck by lightning. There was a hollowed-out area within her branches next to her trunk. The earth was scorched there as well. Leaving my stick outside the entrance I crouched and entered her bosom knowing this was a sacred space. Leaning my back against her rough trunk and nestling my butt into the warm, churned dirt, my arms rested perfectly on two branches coming out from her sides. Sanctuary. The sun burned overhead and under the protection of her branches all I felt was a warm breeze. I rested there, held, feeling the nurturing of the earth as it warmed my feet, my thighs, my loins, rising up my body into the embrace of the juniper tree. Could being with a lover be this kind? Could I receive this much sweetness and allowance of myself? Between my legs the dirt was soft, and I gently inserted the heart rock, two gold coins, and hawk feather, creating a shrine to honor the moment.

-Fragments-

There are many other experiences and lessons on the Ridge that day but most importantly was this: In this beautiful world of ours you will always find what you are looking for. Seek magic, wonder, and possibilities and you shall find them. seek trauma drama and misery and the Earth will give that to you as well. Our planet does not have a point of view about what you choose. It also doesn't have a point of view about whether it has humans on it or not. We can choose whether we would like to live here or completely wipe ourselves off the face of the planet. Perhaps the only demand that the Earth has of us now is that if we truly desire to live here we need to show up now. All of our potency, our consciousness, our awareness, our presence, our gifts, our receiving of ourselves and each other. There is no more time to live in half measures. If you choose life, then choose the glory of all you came here to be. You don't need to know how, that's not your job. Listen, trust yourself, trust your body, trust the earth. Your body will let you know if you're getting off track.

What is the gift you came here to be that no one else can be? What if the greatest gift you can be to the planet is choosing to follow what is joyful for you, even when it doesn't make sense to anyone else? Especially when it doesn't make sense to anyone else!

Or choose mediocrity and slowly decay to death and nothing. For my children, humanities children, and the world that I know is possible, I choose to live.

This is a book with far reaching influence that captures the essence of humanity and nature in a way the invites all who experience it to know themselves better, love their bodies, seek kindness, and honor the energy of change, movement, creation, healing, and miracles.

Healing the earth isn't about healing the earth at all. It's about healing all the places we have created separation between the exquisite knowing of our bodies and the vast awareness of the planet.

I had been to the ridge a couple years before, it called then too... I woke up one morning and felt the rocks in the desert to the east calling "come to me". That day turned out to be one of the most cherished memories of my life- but that is another story.

"Come to me and sing your song..." it called. I had never really gone to such a nice place by myself before. Having been married for so much of my adult life I always seemed to be with someone. Holly, so strange to be here without her.

I removed my clothes and left them in a neat pile next to my backpack. Wearing only my elk-tooth necklace, spiral branch in hand, I stepped through the portal and into the otherworld.

The Golden Waterfall...

Delving my hands into the earth coming back with handful after handful of gold coins. The earth was abundant and rejoiced in gifting to me. A rupture of gold cascading over the edge of the ridge to the valley below.

How do you start a tale when you know you're only in the middle of it? You start in the middle.

Climbing back up the way I had come down years before, erasing the mold of regret I had forged for myself.

You want to heal the earth?? Take your body on a date, ask it questions. Go for a walk in the forest and ask it which way it wants to go. When you wake up take a moment and hold your body, say "hello". Ask: Body, if you could receive anything today, what would it be?? And what would be fun for you today??

Healing the earth has to begin with the part of the earth you actually possess — your Body! Your body knows how to do the rest.

She was the love of my life now lost to another time...

Sleeping under her fallen body with the howling wind rushing over my body I could feel the earth turning under me. Luna, high overhead, gently gracing her path across the night sky, resting in a quilt of stars and planets. Sun, racing under me to see if he could get to the other side before she nestled and disappeared into the irony of dawn.

What if I could erase my choice and everything I decided it meant? Was it even true that I could never catch up to Holly? What was I actually chasing? What if I could undo every significance and separation I had created with that choice? I walked the course in reverse, energetically sweeping away every step, every scream begging for her distant form to wait, every surge of energy as I spurred my body onward knowing it was too little too late to reach her before she crested the hill that I decided was where we needed to meet again.

How many visions have I twisted to my own design? How many prophecies have I tainted with the innocence of my yearning when the earth was inviting me to just Be? I wonder if there is a creative potency that lies there? The energy doesn't lie, you see. Suffering is in the separation between what we want and what is, or is it? What if it's not suffering at all, but the alchemy of body and soul?

Your body is the lens through which your being is creating its reality. Your body is the frequency generator.

And I sang it. I sang it to the sky. I sang it to the neighboring ridges. I sang it to the valley below. I sang it with all my heart, soul, power and vulnerability. I sang to all my lost loves. I sang to my children. I sang to the hidden fears of the shy boy trying to make himself invisible in the corner. I sang to the bitterness of a lost marriage and dream. I sang for freedom and hope in a world full of doubt.

I stood boldly on the edge of the ridge. Drawing the energy of the earth up through my feet settled in the dry dirt, up through my legs, my cock, my abdomen, filling my arms and hands, swelling in my chest. Inhaling a breath to the bottom of my spine and exhaling I rocketed my song through my dry throat into the devouring hot wind. I sang until the breath was gone then digging deep, I sang again. The sound was not pretty. Every wretch and croak tearing from my body sounded as if a dozen of the ragged desert hawks scanning overhead had been gathered in a canvas bag and then beaten against the cliff wall until they were nothing but blood, bone, and feathers. And the song was perfect.

I stood proudly, sun on my naked skin, twisted stick in my hand, feet gripping the earth, arms stretched to the east and west encompassing all, knowing I had accomplished my invitation.

Now I sing the songs of the bodies of the earth. Sometimes they are consonant or dissonant, melodic or caustic, loud or frail, confident or unsure. Sometimes I sound like an ancient shaman or a Tuvan monk. I sing songs that embrace the darkness and songs that remember the joy of youth. The earth calls me and I sing. I have sung in the desert, in an ocean cave as tears dripped from my face, the enchanted woods of my childhood, the top of mountains, a Hawaiian jungle, The Statue of Liberty and the haunted corridors of Ellis Island, and the mystic forests of Vancouver, BC. Every time the song is different; the land has a different message for my body and through my body. Sometimes it is the songs of ancestor's other times a song of hope for the future. And with the beautiful bodies that I work with it is the song of what is. There is no sound to be ashamed of or fear. All of them, no matter what, are an invitation to heal the separation we have created between body and being, body and earth. A teacher of mine said "whatever arises, love that." I sing the song of whatever arises, inviting it into the space of allowance, the kindness of being received and heard.

What is the earth saying to you?

The Author

Ben Noble
www.HealingEarthBook.com/ben-noble

CHAPTER 3

Earth's Magic Healing

Angela Redman

She understood the language in the stillness, in the moment, in the daily rhythms of her experiences; all of them are when she was truly present in her being. Expansion in our bodies, in her body filling up all the minute spaces and places within this blessed, grateful body she had been gifted this lifetime.

The magic received from our divine Earth in which we live upon is so kind, beautiful and simply overwhelming at times at its incredible power, beauty, sacredness and delight. A delight that is so precious and true we cannot ignore its whispers.

Whispers from within the Earths magic are not a random act, of course not. It's continued generosity and natural innate state reveals her offerings to us; how could we possibly comprehend the magnitude of our beautiful planet in one lifetime. Sweetly, kindly and joyfully offers her to us every day, all with no exceptions, no shortages of the divine magic that is continuously participating around us.

How can we embrace this Earth magic healing, restoration and balance from the experience being gifted to us in this blessed human experience? How does Earths magic show up for you each day? I invite you to take the time to see the experience consciously how your Earth's magic presents itself for you and then, more importantly, what are you going to do with it?

How can we quantify within this, our Earth, how generous and precious Earth? I am going to call her she is our only Home! Delicious with many blessings, experiences, healing coming to us each day, each hour, every minute and each second. 24/7 she shows her Earth magic!

Color, brightness, brilliance, panache, which are you choosing to experience? Caring is passed on to each other from our core of her Earth magic. Offered every day to you without question and we cannot help but pass on the brilliance she be.

Our caring, sharing to each other is our natural state of being, just like our Earth magic. She passes in on innately as if we are just part of the team and we continue to unite on the gift of the silent Earth magic.

Take for example, how do you really feel when you are in the presence of a very old tree with its roots imbedded? Feel her, strong, grounded and mighty right? Silently mother Earths magic appears again with open protecting arms above and below you.

How do you feel when you're at the beach, come on, its absolute magic — you know it is. Its water is huge, vast, serene, beautiful and full of life, another miracle of the Earth magic. How does it get any better than this? Well it does, everyday your oceanic experience awaits us. How are you going to choose today from the Earth magic menu?

Do you want something from above, in the middle or below the Earth's crust? She is very flexible and does not discriminate, judge or even say no. She is intelligent; she is constantly doing her job 24/7, focused and coherently sorting, sizing out that which is required of her. It's a mammoth task, seven days a week, with no rest. She loves it so much; it's the pleasure of and the magnitude of perfect rehabilitation of what needs to be done.

We can assist her if we choose to support her ongoing mission of continued balancing of her natural rhythms — she is, we be.

Stillness within is imperative to our being. It's so vital for you and your wellbeing, that when we go within we are tapping into our Earthly magic that is within us. Refreshed, with vast endless and infinite possibilities are to be hard and awaits us. Mother Earth experiences the gifts and challenges like we do. We are synergistically connected to each other and to everyone around us. Even our animals and pets are greatly affected by the ebbs and flows of what happens on our planet Earth.

Our natural nutrition that our Earth provides us, in its many forms, is required if we are absolutely intended to reach that stillness and be rewarded with the bounty of health and well-being benefits along the way.

Mindfulness is the Earth language message from the heart. She wants us to be still, listen and go within. Go within to the space of our own being in mindfulness. She has been speaking to us for a very long time, quietly mostly but not always?

She needs us more than ever to assist her if we are to go forward and heal her back to health. Our path is to contribute to her phenomenal Earth magic that we all know exists. When has this magic ever failed us, we are talking about the incredible intelligence of nature, it has always been present for us to learn, guiding us to a harmonious life with our Earth magic. Listen and you'll hear her, speaking out now to everyone, every living being on this planet that it is time to change and be with her and support her.

The limited thinking through the persistence of greed, power, consumption, accumulation, bigger, better, faster and would you like fries with that attitude! Has led us on an alternate path. The gorge on her precious minerals has created an adrenaline rush for man that can only last for a limited period of time and its continuation would lead to an artificial material addiction. Change is required now.

Our many cultures have learnt great natural wisdom over many millennia; they have passed down their knowledge over time from generation to generation to assist working with Mother Earth's magic. We still have much to learn from the past and unlearn from the present.

Earth continues to pass her knowledge on to us, it's there for us to understand and use to the best of our abilities, with her guidance, to cultivate a connection with our sisters and brothers who we share with this planet with. Unity within our natural surroundings and balancing the giving and receiving with all life forms will have a longer lasting benefit for all. This is the Magic we seek and shall find.

When we are called upon to perform something that really feels very true for us we are infinitely connected to our environment and responding to our highest ideals and callings. This is our Earth magic speaking to us, providing us with the most intuitive revelations.

I invite you to consider your next invitation to the choices you will receive with supporting our mother now and into the future. Do not hesitate, the time to act is now, all positive changes will create new possibilities, we are all in this together.

We are the custodians of our planet; we were given this birthright to help her help our children and our children's children.

Earth, beloved mother, the touch of you, I feel you under me, lying with you, connecting with you, being with you.

Feeling your presence around me, through me and within me.

You with me is me and I you.

I am one with her and all is only one.

The Author

Angela Redman

www.HealingEarthBook.com/angela-redman

CHAPTER 4

The Essence of Being in Communion with the Earth

Luz Adame

Have you ever asked yourself who you really are? And what contribution are you to the planet that you have not yet recognized?

Do you have any idea what contribution you really are to this beautiful planet called Earth and everyone around you?

Did you know that the earth would not be the same if you did not exist or if you ceased to exist? You may think that I am wrong or how could you be a gift to the planet if you have so many problems in your life, in your home, in your marriage and with your children, if you almost cannot pay the rent, cover your basic needs month by month, if your children live in a constant battlefield, if everything you've wanted to do has not been done for some reason or another that you don't even know, if you don't have money in your wallet or bank account, if you did not graduate from school or if you did and you are not practicing or working in your field, if you lack physical beauty, if your body is not beautiful like the models you see in magazines and television, if you have failed again and again in your relationships. How come you could be a gift, right? If your whole life is a failure! And if I told you "YES, YOU ARE A WONDERFUL GIFT", your existence is a wonderful gift!

I will tell you a little bit about me, I am the sixth daughter of a family of eight children, headed by my mother, a single mother, a very talented, smart and courageous woman, who never acknowledged herself on how brilliant she was and who also became an alcoholic in order to deal with all her troubles, pain and suffering, she also became very angry, mean and a violent person when she was drunk. I experience and witness all kinds of physical, emotional and mental abuse from my mother and sexual abuse from close relatives! At some point in my life I believed that I was not worth, or I was not a contribution to anything or anyone in my life. Even I was considering taking my own life, after experiencing violence and control during my marriages. But then I realized that everything was just a lie that I have been telling myself. I realized that despite the childhood I had and not finishing my career, not fitting into my family's reality, having failed in three different relationships, the verbal, emotional and financial abuse that I experienced in my last two relationships. Despite all that, none of that destroyed my essence, my true self. For the contrary, I became a stronger woman with many desires to create something different in my life and contribute to each person that shows up in my life. I have also discovered how the earth has contributed to my life, the animals, the plants and everything around me. I discovered my healing abilities, which I did not know that existed before, because I was only focused on my problems and the negativity that surrounded me. I did not recognize and acknowledge myself as the gift and the contribution I truly am.

Life is the most precious gift that anyone can have, waking up every morning, being able to feel the sun touching our skin, breathing the breeze of the air, the wind delighting us with its wonderful harmonious sound, the smell of the dirt after the rain, the fragrance of the flowers and nature, the song of the birds at the sunrise.

We have everything to live happily, but we do not see it. What is the earth is requesting from us? What is it that the earth is communicating with each earthquake, hurricane, tsunami and all those natural events that we call natural disasters, devastation and death? What is behind all that? Have you ever wondered what the earth requires of you?

Unfortunately, we never ask ourselves that question. When a natural disaster happens, we regret it and see it as a terrible event, but we never ask ourselves what our mother earth requires of each one of us? We are always focused on what we call "our problems", thinking about how to create more material things and we forget to live our life. We forget how beautiful it is to stop for a moment to contemplate a beautiful landscape, to listen to the song of the birds, the sound of the leaves of the trees when dancing with the rhythmic movement of the wind trying to communicate with us. We really forget who we are and why we came to this planet. We forget the essence of being and being in communion with the earth.

You will ask yourself, what is that of the essence of being? Have you ever observed small children, enjoying every moment of their lives, smiling for things that in our eyes are not important or funny, stopping to explore everything around them, jumping, running, playing, laughing loudly, full of life, full of possibilities, full of joy, full of love and gratitude for everything around them, being loving and affectionate... that is the essence of being present, the space of communion with the earth and oneness?

For me it is beautiful to see the children playing in the park, to see how they share, play, and explore with other children, whom they had never seen in their life before, regardless where they come from, origin, race, skin color, language, social status. Among children there is uniqueness, glory, joy and harmony, happiness. Being is what the mother earth requires of us.

Let's stop hurting, hating, judging, envying each other. The earth is abundant and full of gratitude for each one of us. The earth shares all it is, and we do not see it, or we do not want to see it and receive it. When there is a natural disaster is the only way we are willing to unite and see how valuable life is and after the chaos ends, we forget and function again from a space of contraction, violence, judgments and competition and that is how we are raising our children.

What do we need to change here? What the earth is requiring of us that we are not being? What is the earth crying out loud? The earth is very generous and gentle with us, it only gives us a wake-up call when creating a natural disaster, where there are human losses, but it is only to get our attention. We forget that the planet earth is so powerful, it is like when your mother calls your attention when you are not behaving properly, and she is demanding a change from you. That is what the earth is doing with us when it's expressed in some way; it is demanding a change of each one of us.

What are we doing all day inside our homes, inside our work day by day, forgetting to be happy? What if the earth only requires that we operate from a space of ease, joy and glory? From a space of uniqueness, of communion with the earth.

What if you go for a walk to the closest park from your house, take of your shoes, feel the grass caressing your feet, and feel as the sun caress your skin. Listen to the song of the birds and the leaves of the trees dancing to the rhythm of the wind, creating an orchestra that delights your ears, enjoying that space of harmony, of communion with the earth. It's just a choice!

When, I function from a space of despair, anxiety, anger or sadness. I go for a walk to the park and I allow myself to receive everything that nature offers me, I take off my shoes, walk on the grass with my bare feet, hug a tree and ask it to contribute to me with its energy. It only takes a few minutes for all those feelings to go away, and my body and my being are invaded by a feeling of harmony, of possibilities and of joy. This is an invitation that I would like to make to all of you. Even if you live in a big city, full of buildings and pavement, look for a park, look for a green area full of nature! And allow yourself to receive all of what the nature wants to contribute to you, flooding you with all the possibilities that are available to you and that are only waiting for you to say "Yes", and that you are willing to receive. You will never know if it works, if you never try it! You must be willing to experience new things to know if they work for you, otherwise you will never know if it works. It's just a choice!

I'm going to tell you an experience about my life that happened last summer. It was a beautiful and warm Sunday morning; my children were on vacation and my sister was visiting us from Mexico and she was staying a few days in our house. That morning I had planned to work at home. Suddenly, while I was working my sister and brother invited me to spend a family day on the beach with them, and of course I answered no, because I had plans and wanted to work. They didn't take "No" as an answer, and they said cordially and with a smile on their faces "yes, you're coming". And I was not very happy to accept it, but I was very angry all the way because I felt compelled to go with them and felt I was doing something I did not want to do, according to my point of view. Well, when we arrived at the beach, I took my shoes off and started walking on the sand and I took a deep breath, and my body totally relaxed and all that feelings of discomfort I had went away as if by magic. It was something wonderful and I recognized that it was crazy not wanting to go to the beach to have fun when I was invited to have a good time, to be with my family, to enjoy the sound of the sea, the breeze, the sand, the rays of the sun caressing my skin. At that moment I understood that in many areas of my life I have been invited to play and I have refused to play, to be alive and enjoy every moment of my life. It is crazy when we operate from that space in which we deny ourselves the pleasure of having fun for all the responsibilities we have, and we refuse to play. I would like to invite you to ask yourself in what areas of your life are you refusing to play and have fun like when you were a child. Many times, we make excuses like we have very important things to do, and we prefer to stay at home, most of the time we do not do anything that we were supposed to do, and we do not accept the invitation to go out and have fun.

Sometimes when we get in to our heads, we forget all the amazing things this planet is offering us. We want to figure out everything with our heads, we forget how amazing is the space when we are in the presence of nature. We spend hours, days, months, years inside our homes waiting just to die, forgetting how amazing is the world outside, in contact with nature. How you ever experienced how it feels hugging a tree? To walk with your bare feet on the grass? On the sand?

That is what I do when I'm getting into what I call the rabbit whole, that space of darkness, depression, no possibilities, anger, rage and fury, and hate for not having what I said I want to have, for not being what I think I want to be and that I'm not. When I get cutup into other people's realities, judgments and limitations and I make them as mine.

By spending a few minutes in contact with nature and having communion with the earth you will start to create a new space of possibilities,

possibilities that you did not know where there before, because you couldn't see them with all those walls you had put up. When you focus in your problems is all you can see, but when you allow yourself to be and receive everything the earth is willing to contribute to you, all those walls of separation start to fall off and you will start to perceive, know, be and receive everything around you.

I have a friend that has been struggling with his body's health for a very long time. When he is at home his body starts to ache and he starts to become depress, but as soon as he goes to the beach and play in the ocean, he becomes a completely different person and his whole body becomes happy and full of life. He and his body love been in the ocean surfing, and with each wave he rides he allows himself to be in communion with the earth and receives, and enjoy everything the earth is gifting him. He is willing to receive the nurturing healing that the Earth gives him every time he chooses to be in communion with the Earth.

You're probably asking yourself, "How would you know when you are in communion with the earth?" And "how can you get there?"

Lest play a little exercise that I learned a few years ago from Access Consciousness®! Are you ready? Ok, then...

Please close your eyes and take a deep breath in from the top of your head down to the tips of your toes allowing yourself to relax with each deep breath in you take in, and thanking your body and your being for been the gift that you are, allowing yourself to expand in all directions including down into the earth, and expand even more, ten thousand miles more in all directions , and even bigger than that, and expand one hundred thousand miles in all directions including down into the earth connecting with the core of planet earth and ask the earth. Earth what contribution am I to you? And allow the earth to receive the energetic contribution you are to it by connecting with the earth and being everything, you truly are that you haven't acknowledge. And then ask Earth what contribution are you to me that I haven't acknowledge? And allow yourself to receive everything the earth is contributing to you creating that connection with the earth by been in communion with the earth. And continue to expand even bigger than what you already expanded and even bigger than that, and bigger than the universe and continue to gift and receive the energetic contribution you are to the earth and the earth is to you and from that space, you can open your eyes when you are ready.

How is your body doing? How do you perceive yourself after this exercise? How do you perceive the earth now? You can practice this exercise any time you would like to and everywhere you go. I love to do this exercise every time I go to the park, but you can do it everywhere, just play with it and see what shows up for you!

I love to connect with the earth using this amazing Access Body Process created by Mr. Gary Douglas and Dr. Dain Heer the founder and co-founder of Access Consciousness®, this body process is called **Restoration of Communion with Earth™** which is an Access hands on Body Process that invites you to have a conversation and communion with the Earth, your body, your life and more. This is a Body Process you can learn in an Access Consciousness® Body Process class.

I used this Access hands on body process with my mother when she was very ill in the hospital in Mexico City back in February 2015. A day before I arrived at Mexico from Long Beach, CA where I live, all my family members went to visit my mother because she was dying, and the doctors told them that she just had some hours left. When I got to the hospital the next morning I couldn't believe how she looked, her eyes had lost the light of life and they look so opaque, she look very weak and tired, I just couldn't recognize her. When she saw me, she said "you came!" I had to hold my tears back, so she didn't notice them, I asked, "mom is there anything I can contribute to you? Would you please allow me to contribute to you?" She replied "yes", and then I went to reach the sole of her feet and ask the energy of the Access Consciousness® Body Process "**Restoration of Communion with Earth™**" to run on her body.

Honestly, I didn't know what to expect out of it, I just wanted to contribute to her in her dying process. I also asked my body to contribute to her body with whatever she required for her have more ease. I ran this body process for about an hour before my sister asked me to allow my other sister that just arrived from Los Angeles to come up to see my mother. In Mexico, only one person is allowed to be in the room with the patient (in the hospital). So, before I left, I was able to see the magic that this body process created on my mother's body. The look on her face changed completely and her eyes had become shiny again with a sparkle of life. I told my mother before I left the room "I am coming back at night to stay with you," and then I left.

Later on, I heard comments from family members that went to see her a day before to say goodbye to her that they couldn't believe how good my mom looked the next day, that it was a miracle and maybe the doctors gave her a medication that assisted her to get better.

When I came back to the hospital that night, my mom was totally awake, and she looked so good. So, I asked her "if she would allow me to contribute to her" and she replied "yes", and I ran again the energy of **Restoration of Communion with Earth™** on the sole of her feet.

She didn't mention anything to me, but she told my sister that was taking care of her during the day "I don't know what your sister Luz did to me, but I feel so good". That created so much joy in my universe.

After that my mom was released from the hospital on the middle of February, I came back to the United States on late February and she lived until May 12, 2017. She passed away after accomplishing all the things she wanted to take care of. She died from complications of the radiotherapy she received as a treatment of a cancerous tumor she had, she was cancer free at the time she passed.

Why did I bring up this story? Before I went to Mexico I didn't completely acknowledge myself as I contribution and I didn't believed so much in my healing capacities. My visit to Mexico was an amazing contribution to my life and to stop doubting myself.

We all have amazing healing capacities, but must of the time we don't know it, or we refused to know it!

I had another experience with a young bird my brother rescued out of a cat's mouth, this was back in 2014. My brother was coming home from work and he noticed the neighbor's cat had something in its mouth, after noticing that it was a little bird that was still alive he took it away from the cats' mouth and he noticed that this little bird was injured under his winds, there were wounds made by the cats' fangs. The bird was very weak, my brother took it inside his apartment, he showed it to his wife and she was trying to assist it and feed it. The bird was not responding. That day I visited my brother and I asked his wife if she would allow me to hold the bird in my hands, and in my mind, I asked the little bird, is there anything I can contribute to you? I don't have any point of view of what you want to choose, but If there is anything I can assist you with please receive it from me. Then I requested the energy of Access Consciousness® Body Process **"Restoration of Communion with Earth™"** to run on its body and I said, "Whatever you required from my body to heal your body please take it. If you choose to die I don't have any point of view".

After running this energies on the bird's body for about an hour or so, he stated to move, and I wet my finger with water and rubbed it on the bird's beak, I did it several times until the bird started to open its beak then I took some drops water and put them inside its beak, at this point the bird started to drink the water, then I took small pieces of wet crumbs of bread and the bird started to eat.

Then the little bird started to look okay, and I placed it on my shoulder and I could perceive its gratitude. I could perceive the connection that was created between us.

I would like to invite you to look in to your own life for events that you had experience that will remind you the gift and the contribution you had been with people, animals, plants and the earth. All the magic you had created that you haven't acknowledge.

Below there are some questions you can ask. These questions would give you the awareness of the contribution you are to the earth and everyone and everything on it and it will assist you to start changing everything that is not working for you in your life. When you ask questions, you are not looking for an answer what you are looking for, is the awareness that would create something greater in your life because, questions empower you and answers disempowered you. Asking questions will start to open doors of possibilities you never knew existed before. What if who you think you are it is a total lie?

- What would happen if I started to acknowledge myself as the gift I truly am?

- What would happen if I let go of the past? What would that create for me and planet earth?

- What contribution am I that I have not yet recognized because I am living in the past?

- What would I create if I let go of the past and start acknowledging me as the contribution I truly am to everybody around me and to the earth?

- What gift am I refusing to be when I am choosing to play small? Who am I being? In whose reality am I trying to fit in?

- Earth what gift and contribution am I to you that I haven't acknowledge?

- What Energy, Space and Consciousness can me and my body be to perceive, know, be and receive the contribution I truly be to the earth and everyone and everything around me?

- What questions are we not asking?

- What contribution are we to the planet earth that we haven't acknowledge?

- What can we receive from the earth that we are not receiving?

- If I choose to let go of the limitations I have made so real and true in my life, what would that create?

- What energy, space and consciousness can me and my body be that would allow us to be in total communion with the earth?

- If I choose to be joyful instead of trauma and drama what would that change?

- How much space can I occupy that would allow me to be the space of being I truly be?

- What is required of me to create a better life on planet earth?

- How can we contribute to each other?

- What else can I choose that I am not choosing?

- What have I made so vital about creating separation from planet earth with the trauma and drama I am choosing?

- What choice can I make today that would contribute the energy that the earth requires from me?

- What is truly possible to create in planet earth?

- How the earth is contributing to us that we refuse perceive, know, be and receive?

- What am I refusing to perceive from planet earth?

- How can I change everything that is not working on planet earth?

- What else is truly possible that we haven't acknowledge?

- How many lies am I using to create the limitations and disconnection from me and planet earth I am choosing?

- What would it take from me to function from the space of being I truly be and connect with planet earth with ease, joy and glory?

- If I truly choose to function from the space of being what will that create?

- What invitation can I be to others to expand and awaken the consciousness in everyone and everything in planet earth?

- What possibilities are now available to me that didn't existed before?

- Is my pain and suffering contributing to planet earth? Earth what do you require of me? Do you require my pain and suffering?

- If I choose to close of the back doors I have open to stop myself from choosing more consciousness what would that create?

- How many lies am I using to create the unconsciousness and anti-consciousness on planet earth?

- How many lies am I buying from others to keep in place the unconsciousness and anti-consciousness on planet earth?

- What energy, space and consciousness can me and my body be to be the space of being me and my body truly be for all eternity?

- How much space can I occupy today that would allow me to have more of me?

- Your willingness to ask questions would start to create the change you can create for you and your life.

- How many times are we refusing to enjoy the beauty the earth is offering us? Putting all kind of excuses in front of us giving reasons and justifications for why we cannot enjoy our lives.

- My invitation to you is to explore other possibilities that will bring more joy into your life and will allow you to perceive, know, be and receive everything that is available to you and start to create a greater life and living by being in communion with the Earth and everyone and everything on it.

- What other choices can you make today that you haven't allow yourself to make because you don't want to be judge for choosing different?

- Would you be willing to be everything you can be that you haven't allow yourself to be? Would you be willing to be all of YOU? Would you be willing to be as different as you are?

- Would you dare to hug a tree and ask for its contribution? Would you be willing to receive it all?

Only you can choose something different...

After all is just a Choice.

The Author

Luz Adame

www.HealingEarthBook.com/luz-adame

CHAPTER 5

One Tree

Sylvia Remington

Driving from my parent's house, a huge swooping hawk caught my eye as it glided through the air, dancing on the air waves, soaring with the wind from mountain to mountain amidst the valley. Its movement bespoke an ease and freedom and communion with everything around it.

I pulled over to the side of the road and almost held my breath to watch it. So beautiful and simple and majestic and free and spacious. And wow, how he flew! It was truly breathtaking to witness the beauty of nature, and this amazing creature interacting with it. In this moment, watching the hawk being himself, I got back to being present with me. I'm so grateful for it. It reminded me that I have that ability to create this same space in my world. Thank you, sweet hawk, teacher and friend.

Earlier that day, I drove past an old apartment complex that I used to live in, and I saw they were chopping down all the trees. When I pulled over and asked what was going on, the apartment landlord stated plainly, "It takes too much money to water these hundred-year-old trees and plants, so we stopped watering them. And now we're cutting them down. We're in the desert, for goodness sakes!"

My heart sank.

My mind raced.

I wondered about what else I could do.

I even asked myself, "What can I do?" The question repeated in my head almost like a mantra with no end... "What can I do? What can I do? What can I do?" And I got, in that moment, nothing. But I also was aware that this didn't mean there was nothing I could do in the future. So, I kept asking questions. I knew deep down that if I kept asking questions about what else was and is possible, something amazing would show up and make itself known to me.

A week later, I drove by the apartment complex, and more trees were being chopped down. Again, I asked: What can I do with this? Can I change it? And if so, how do I change it? (Questions that I've heard asked in classes I've taken with Access Consciousness.)

Once again, I got, "Wait for now. There is nothing you can do in these 10 seconds."

Even though I heard this again, I knew I wouldn't stop asking questions. I wasn't going to give up. I knew, deep down within me that there was SOMETHING or some contribution I could be for this situation. I perceived the trees so strongly. And I KNEW somehow, I could be a contribution to them... even if it was going to show up totally differently than I had planned or thought it would show up.

Another week passed. As I was driving home from my night shift at a retail store, my hands suddenly turned the wheel of the car so that I was driving a different direction than I normally commuted home. My body took over and its awareness and consciousness brought me to my old apartment complex.

All the trees had been chopped down except for one.

I knew, in that moment, that I could contribute in some way. And I could contribute to the tree.

If I had spent any time over-thinking this whole situation, I may have convinced myself to drive away. I mean, it was 10:30pm at night! I could have worried about what people would think of me walking in this area at this time of night... And this thought crossed my mind for a nano-second; however, I brushed that musing aside, and got out of the car. The last tree standing was calling to me. I perceived I could contribute in some way. And to me, this is what mattered. No matter how many people thought I was crazy, it didn't matter. Doubt fell away as I knew I could gift something to this tree; and somehow, I knew that this offering had the potential to create a ripple effect for more possibilities on the planet.

As I got out of my car and walked past the newly chopped stumps, I put my hands on them, touching each one. Acknowledging each one. Saying thank you for the life they had created on this planet. And as my hands lightly moved over them, sawdust stuck to my fingers and sifted through my hands. I kept walking... stepping over the fallen limbs and branches of the trees. Acknowledging each one, I kept walking.

Until I got to the last tree. Most of her branches were chopped off. But she was still alive and vibrant. I heard her whisper to me, "I'm not ready to go." I placed my hands on her and said, "Whatever I can contribute, I contribute to you now." I felt this humming/buzzing of energy flow through my body, as if my molecules were vibrating and I was vibrating with the energy of life. I perceived the energy of the earth, reaching up from deep within the soil to meet this beautiful tree and to meet me. It was this incredible energy of connection to the earth, and a simultaneity of gifting and receiving between myself, the tree, nature, and the earth. There are almost no words for this experience. It was such a communion of energy with the earth that my whole being came alive. I perceived the energy of me. And it was a beautiful, energetic conversation. The energy of a communication without words. It was such a vibrant way to speak.

I said to the tree, "I'm aware they will be cutting you downtomorrow. You still have choice. You can leave your body and find another tree to inhabit. You can go now beforetomorrow. And there are so many other possibilities. I know a body process I can do for you that can contribute to the change you are experiencing too. And whatever I can do to contribute, I will. I am so grateful for you. I love you and I won't forget you." I left my hands on the tree a bit longer, perceiving her greatness and how much she was such a gift to me. The thick, layered bark beneath my hands pulsated and radiated with a sparkly, scintillating, vibrating, effervescent, loving and light-filled beautiful energy. I thanked her. And when it was time, I took my hands off.

The tree then directed me to one of her branches that had been already chopped down and was lying beside her. She told me, I could take this part of her home with me to keep the awareness of her spirit alive. It was an honoring of the gift of me and the gift of her.

And so, I did.

Since that night, I've driven by, and I see that her body is gone. But her spirit is not. And I still have the beautiful walking stick of a branch.

In the space where the tree once occupied, I sometimes now see the hawk flying and gliding and dancing. The hawk's gentleness, potency, vulnerability, and presence in total communion with nature. It soars amongst the energies that are still ever present. It circles and flies high up. Moving, creating with the wind, landing on trees that are still in this world, and being present with the earth. Watching the hawk, I realize, I am the hawk and the hawk is me. And I can tap into this at any time.

What else can I be to be this amazing hawk energy, in total communion with nature and being the gift, I am to the world I know is possible? And how can we each be more kind, nurturing for the planet, the world, and the earth? What else is possible with this? What else does it take to create dynamic change in the world? And is this the change we've been asking for? What questions, choices, energy, space and consciousness can we each BE to create with our gifts and with the earth? What ripple can your being BE on the planet?

What truly is possible with our capacities, our gifts, healing, and the earth?

~ ~ ~ ~ ~ ~ ~ ~ ~ ~ ~ ~ ~ ~ ~ ~

Some tools I use to connect with the earth... (in case you'd like to play with some of these)

1. Breathe in the beautiful fresh air that the trees are contributing/ providing; and release out and melt away any heavy energies from your body to be dissipated into the earth (which the earth will use as nourishment, regrowth, and fertilizer for more! How does it get any better than that?!).

2. Connect with the earth below, and reach out and connect with the universe above. Perceive the energy of the earth beneath your feet, and touch the natural world below you and around you gently with your hands. Then reach your hands to the sky and perceive that infinite space and energy radiating to you and from you.

3. Ask questions about the world around you and within you with a sense of wonderment.

4. What would be fun and joyful for you? What can you do today to play with the earth? And laugh with the earth? What communion can you be with the earth today? Even if it's just a brief little walk, perceiving the trees and the wind as you move through space. This can become a nature meditative walk, even if it is for a few moments. :)

5. Ask: what do you know about nature and the earth that no one else knows, that could contribute to the change you know is possible with the earth? And truly, what else is possible?

I realize healing, peace, kindness, joy and love are all around us and within us.

So, what do you choose and create?

We are each so amazing and have such breathtaking gifts to contribute to the planet. Thank you for you being you. You are amazing. And I'm so grateful for you reading this. Thank you.

The Author

Sylvia Remington

www.HealingEarthBook.com/sylvia-remington

CHAPTER 6

A Fairie Tale

Shellie Padilla

Long ago, before there were humans, the fairies lived in a magical place that was full of majesty and great wonder. There was a blissful, harmonious **TENALACH** (a deep connection that makes you one with nature) among all things in creation on this holy ground. God made the fairies as the angels of nature. They were/are beings of pure, divine light and love with a difficult, but important, mission of healing and protecting the environment and animals. This special place was home to the most natural, unimaginable, timeless beauty that no word could ever describe. It was a diverse playground of wondrous mountains, impressive rolling hills of luxurious emerald green velvet, canyons so deep and wide carved from the landscapes of time in colors and hues unknown to man, dazzling rivers, turquoise seas and oceans, desserts with expansions as far as the eye could see and dense forests which decorated the foreground of the sun's contribution to this serene, picturesque masterpiece. Strategically inhabited by 30 million living species of mammals, birds, amphibians, reptiles, fish, invertebrates, fungi, plants, algae and numerous other organisms, this vast paradise was an intricately woven web of unlimited possibility and manifestation in eternal, unchanging consciousness. This enlightened time and space, represented by an infinite and relentless universal love, was considered, and righteously called, Heaven. Today, the human rendition of this Divine holy ground is called **HEMO-TERRA**... Blood of the Earth... an anthropogenic modification and deconstruction of the earth's surface to better suit the needs of the human population. **THERE IS A SILENT ILLUSIONARY MIS-CONCEPTION AND SENSE OF ENTITLEMENT THAT THE EARTH BELONGS TO MAN.**

For 4.6 billion years Mother Earth has joyfully been supporting and nurturing the blossoming of her inhabitants with tolerance and forgiveness richly laced in patience and unconditional love. She has selflessly sacrificed her planetary characteristics to honor the human race in the name of PROGRESS. In doing so, all other creations have fallen in subservient compliance to human behaviors and have greatly and sorrowfully suffered; some even to their own tragic demise and extinction. The Earth's celebratory rejoices have been muted in poignant melancholy. Her messages have fallen on deaf ears and her sweet symphonic song has been statically echoed back to her in ignorant disregard for her power and intelligence. She has endured horrific inflictions of abuse, yet her manifested blessings exceed all the materialisms mankind can conceivably conjure into existence. Her contributions exceed her debilitations. Her abundant gifts are the tendrils that keep all things connected and, therefore, alive.

Before 500 A.D., man had a good relationship with Mother Earth. Man was in communion with nature. Man did not impose his own will at the detriment of the whole. Man communicated with the great earth spirits as well as the spirits of the heavens through the sun, the moon and the stars and understood the importance of the co-relations between the phases of the moon, the seasons and the tides. Kinship with all the creatures of the earth, sky and water was a real and active principle. The animals and all living organisms had the respect, honor and protection of man. The concept of life, the mystery of living it and its relations provided reverence that all things had the right to live, the right to multiply, the right to freedom and the right to man's indebtedness. All things in existence had equal importance to all. There was mindfulness and a "knowing "of connectedness. Resonating at the same frequency as Mother Earth, and congruent to man's vibrations, beneficent universal consciousness facilitated symmetry across the fascia of the earth. **MAN BELONGED TO THE EARTH.**

There is a place underneath the conscious mind, below the instinctual self, where one's usual identity is dissolved into a blissfully pure witness, observing each experience from a completely detached perspective. All apparent boundaries between self and others disappear... there is no sense of self separate from the whole... what remains is an unadulterated awareness, specific to each individual, but at the same time expanded into the elegant exquisiteness of the boundless and timeless universe. It is within this oneness, this willingness to unleash the bonds of personal convention and societal restraint, that the self can freely acknowledge that it is part of something greater than itself.

In the awareness of the depths and dimensions of earth's magical congruency of man and all else which is encompassed in the space we share, we open to the healing powers associated with all kingdoms, realms and biofields. Every living creature and natural element (such as water and rocks) that dwells within the earth's dominion has a gift to offer to the other. Along with the power to heal one another, each has a guardian angel... a fairie to protect and guide. Fairies rule over the flowers, plants, rocks, stones, crystals, water and all living beings. They are responsible for the therapeutic effect related to nature and the outdoors; hence the reason we become more conscious and vibratory when we are one with nature. It is then that we are able to surrender to the vast concatenation that is the essence of our being. It is within this state of nirvana that we appreciate with magnitude the **DIDIRRI**; the concept of inner deep listening and quiet still awareness, a "tuning-in" experience to deeply understand the captivating and natural beauty this earth gifts to us on a daily basis. When we purposely allow our consciousness to unfold into the ripples of energetic life, the synapses between reality and the exuberant expression of perception dissipates allowing who we truly BE to step forward with a grand entrance and a participatory nature. We breathe the cool, refreshing air with deeper breaths. We see colors with a vibrancy and authenticity that we have never NOTICED before. We smell the exotic and captivating fragrances of nature that are foreign to us in our waking world... like PETRICHOR; the fresh earthy smell after it rains. If we listen, we will hear the grand symphony conducted by nature's choir. We touch the land and its bountiful offspring from which we can eat the most delicious and delectable berries, fruits, mushrooms, grasses and herbs of every form unscathed by the human hand. That which we have escaped from is that which brings our being into balance and accord. That which we destroy is that which the earth has provided us for sustainability, wholeness and well-being during our human experience. Our fairies carry special panacea energies. They have the power to heal all our man-made and self-inflicted ailments, especially those associated with the heart. They help us understand our place in the world and the symbolic rhythms of nature. They help us understand the aspects of life that our ancestors knew instinctively and intuitively. Fairies carry our prayers and affirmations to the angels and the higher realms; they encourage and increase our mental prowess and intuitive abilities, creative imagination and inspirations. It is through the efforts and energies of the fairies that partial healing can be achieved for Mother Earth.

The fairies, along with Mother Earth, have long felt the effects of mankind's sequestration upon the earth. The human time span on this globe is relatively short compared to other species, yet, humans assume complete control over all things through systems of oppression and extortion with a superior, self-serving, self-righteous and self-absorbed attitude of privilege which is supposed to quantify and justify their actions unto each other and unto the diverse lands, waters and animals in which they should ultimately be in communion with. Fairies hear the private cries from the womb of our world. The human presence that was once a contribution has become an impediment. This impediment leaches over into the likelihood of human extinction through ignorance and choice. The cycle of destruction in the name of progress mirrors the same destruction to man through disease and sickness. That which is created in and of the world is created in and of the human being. Not only is Mother Earth being depleted of her resources and plant and animal families, she is at risk of being depleted of her human family as well. Mankind has not listened or heeded the tumultuous warnings. The diminished realm of fairies has lost frequency with the hearts of man. They have united forces with the deities and entities of the earth, as well as other worlds and universes, and are consciously choosing to incarnate. By becoming embodied in human form, these humanoids can then go forth into the world and help raise the vibrations of humanity. Mother Earth is requiring this in order to mend the damages and disconnections, not only with Mother Earth, but also with the lifeblood of the planet... water. Man's inhumanity to the earth, man's inhumanity to the animals, man's inhumanity to the air we breathe and the waters that flow through us that ultimately give us life... man's inhumanity to all things, including man's inhumanity to man, has not gone unnoticed. Man has forgotten the universal law... to love all things; to find love in everything and every situation.

Humanoids come in through the birthing process not remembering who they were before. They come in with a passion for healing the earth, the waters and the human race. They come in for creating unity with all eternity. Humanoids have come to evolve the planet to a higher resonation of BEING. Now is the time for all universes to come to the aid of the quest for interplanetary shifting. Now is the time for the cosmic energies, which are now available to us, to transform that which does not serve these shifts in consciousness. Now is the time for our planet to expand, transition and align with the changes of the universe. Now is the time for mankind to awaken, acknowledge, receive, surrender, connect and BE. **NOW IS THE TIME**.

The finely-balanced and life-supporting frequencies intended to uphold life on the planet communicate oneness like never before. The messages coming through are clear, precise and authoritative. They are not to be taken lightly. We are living in exceptional times... times of manifestation, hope, cleansing, resurrection... times of reuniting with our own divine nature. Love one another. Respect and honor one another. Be indebted to one another, to life, the lifeblood, the animals and plants, the earth and all it holds and implies.

The fairies, angels, deities and entities know and emanate the energies of oneness. The "incarnates" are here to teach us what we have forgotten. Like the fairies, we have the divine power to heal. Our mission should be to heal and protect the environment and animals. Open your hearts to perceive and receive. To become more enlightened... meditate. To become in heart resonance with the endless treasures of the Natural Kingdom... converse with the nature spirits. To uplift the consciousness of all beings globally... radiate positive energies outward through focused thought. To connect... match your nature to earth's nature. To heal your inner self... walk barefoot in nature, breathe the air, listen to the grand symphony conducted by nature's choir and open your eyes to really see the beauty and elegance of everything, from the tiniest leaf to the most gigantic tree, and all that is in between. To remedy the earth... mend mankind. To heal the earth... unite mankind.

Earth healing is not about healing a being that is much greater and more expansive than us. It is about healing us. It is about healing all that we are connected to through the conception of oneness. It is a collective planetary being. It is a universal being. It is a multidimensional being. It is an infinite and eternal being. It is the spark that became the being. It is BEING. What if the Being that you Be could change the world? What if "long ago" could be right now? **WHAT IF HEAVEN COULD BE ON EARTH AGAIN?**

The Author

Shellie Padilla
www.HealingEarthBook.com/shellie-padilla

CHAPTER 7

Healing the Earth through Communion

Deepa Ramaraj

> *"If you really wish to heal the Earth - could you start by laughing more?"* – Gary Douglas, Founder, Access Consciousness

Would the Earth be happy if the people residing on it were sad, upset, angry, fighting and were in total disharmony? My perspective about healing the Earth is that is possible through greater communion within our inner self, with people around us and by then including a peaceful communion with the Earth too. For greater communion with our inner self, I also think it is required to have a greater communion with our body. If my body is sick, to me it mostly means just before that period of sickness, I was choosing to be disconnected with the Earth, with my body and I was in some turmoil on the emotional level. I share here my thoughts on how we could create a greater communion with the Earth and contribute to healing the Earth.

Disconnection from the earth

I was personally disconnected from the Earth for a long time. In my perspective this type of disconnection keeps the Earth from healing and it keeps people away from communion with the Earth, and it keeps us from communion with the universe through the Earth.

So, what is the reason for disconnection from the Earth? For some people it could be the physical abuse meted out to animals or to their own body or others' bodies. To others it may be the way Earth has been abused. For some others it could be the emotional and mental abuse they have suffered which is the source of their disconnection from the Earth.

So here were my questions a few years ago: "Is it that I yearn for a perfect environment that doesn't exist? Could it be that the disharmony that seems to exist in the world as anger, rage disturbs me? What is my reason for disconnection with the Earth and can that be changed?"

Some things that came to me with asking those questions was that I seemed to be waiting to leave the Earth to go to some place of ease and peace. Where is this fairy land of peace, joy and ease? What if there is currently no such place available to me? What if my only choice was to convert this Earth to a place of peace and ease? Would I then be willing to choose to create peace here? Rather than look to find peace outside of me, would I be willing to create peace it inside of me and then allow that to flow outward?

When I asked these questions to myself a few years ago, I was in a state of conflict and in a state of some panic too, I admit. "What? Is there no peaceful place to go to? Would that be a figment of my imagination? There must be other options!" I said to myself.

I allowed myself to be in that state of denial for some weeks. A few weeks of inner struggle ensued, along with a refusal to have ease. I was rebelling within, like a teenager dealing with adulthood and yet unwilling to let go of childhood. This wasn't new to me. I had been in a state of denial for some years — in a state of bewilderment or being puzzled is probably closer to what I had been dealing with. "What am I here on the earth for? What is life about? I love my friends and family — but I hate it here!". But "this state" was different. For the first time I had asked myself — "What if I had no choice? Would I then be willing to create the Earth as a place of ease and peace for me?" And that had taken me to an uncomfortable place of staring at myself in the mirror and asking questions. Questions that I didn't wish to deal with. Questions I wished I could escape.

That was a period a few years ago when I moved from a place of niggling health issues plus a stint of low self-esteem to a space I had created some amount of peace within me. I could see that. Yes, I had used a bunch of tools to create that ease. I looked at the methods I had used to create that peace within me. Could I use the same to spread a little of that peace across the world — at least could a drop of that create a ripple? Yes, I could do that!

Just acknowledging that possibility put me into a whole different way of being. My relationship to me, my relationship to my body, to people and to the world shifted. Today my relationship with the Earth has stepped into greater ease. I am still unlearning my old ways and learning new ways to communicate with the Earth.

I share here the ways I had chosen to create a bit of ease with the Earth. My little way of contributing to the Earth and perhaps healing it too. And if this can change anything for you, I truly wish that it creates a ripple that will heal more people and thus the Earth too.

Step 1: Creating ease with the body

A few years ago, I was dealing with some health issues. The health issues were minor in nature, yet of high nuisance value. One example is that I had a lot of aches and pains in the body. In particular, in my palm — each finger and palm bone joint used to pain. If I bought a phone in those days, to check the suitability I had to physically hold possible new phones in my palm and check whether my palm would ache if I held it! Too heavy was a problem for me and so was too light! Too narrow and too wide used to cause discomfort for my palm too! At that time, I was employed as a manager at a global Information Technology company. I was quite busy at work and apart from this, I was a mother of 2 children managing their meals, tracking homework submissions, hobbies, et al. I was getting the interiors done up for 2 houses. We had rented out our other house in another country. Having a hundred balls up in the air was the norm as I juggled them daily, taking care not to drop any of the hundred balls! Being unwell was not acceptable to me. It was wrongness and in fact I was ashamed that I had any health issues.

I once dialogued with my body and said, "Hey, what is this about? I have treated you well. I have given you a massage or a pedicure once in a while. So, how come this?" My body replied, "And what about the stress you piled on me, the emotional issues you didn't let go of?". As I wondered about that, my whole life came up visually in front of me, a bit like a movie trailer. Oops, yes! Life had been stressful. I had neither been taught to let go, nor had I created any tools to let go of stuff. It wasn't that I planned to stock it up. It was just that I often re-called a string of events that caused emotional pain to me. It seemed that my body was protesting against the stress caused to it.

Any event or incident or dialogue we recall is because we stored it in our body. Our body stores a lot of stuff when we are unwilling to let things go. We make it our trash can. We love to empty the garbage bins of our homes daily. Yet we don't know how to empty the garbage of thoughts, emotions and traumatic memories from our body.

I was determined to get my body repaired of its aches and pains, and other health issues I initially used Pranic Healing and later used Ac-cess Bars and Body processes on my body and within a few months the aches and pains dissolved. My self-confidence began to mend as I started to move around more easily I could pick up things easily, and buy a phone online without testing phones in my hand, without worrying that the palms would ache! The benefits were so liberating for me that I chose to become an Internationally Certified Facilitator for Access Consciousness.

As I began to have more ease with my body, I saw the benefits of emo-tional healing alongside.

Step 2: Creating ease within me

In my perspective, creating ease within me helped me enormously to connect to myself. This step was initially in tandem with Step 1. I soon realised that 'Creating ease within me' is a lifelong process. I now work on emotionally letting go every few days, every few hours and every few minutes — as and when required. If I am in turmoil, mentally or emotionally, I am not connected with who I am. I am not connected with my body. And there is no way I could think of connection to the Earth at such times.

When I am upset, do I even consider the Earth? Or am I busy with the story of my life that is not working for me?

Which species has the maximum presence and impact on the Earth — we do! If we are discontent, would that be healing the Earth? When we are in disharmony within ourselves how much can we connect to the earth?

Louise Hayes work had been an inspiration for me since a long time. She had created a mapping of physical issues with an emotional source. Access also suggests something similar. I found that the Access tools to clear an emotional issue were amazing. I started to look at the emotions that were coming up for me and for others whenever a physical symptom came up. And I started to ask questions, "What message is the body giving? What can be done about this? Can this be changed? If so, how can it be changed?"

Step 3: Creating ease with creating my life

It wasn't as if I wasn't creating my life in childhood, adolescence and afterward. In adolescence I was motivated by studies. Later on, I had various ways to be motivated at work. I was motivated by the work I was doing. I was willing to work hard and work smart to progress in my career. I was willing to save money, invest and create more. When my children were born, something changed for me. I loved spending time with them. My barriers got lowered; I was willing to be vulnerable with them. I was more willing to see whether I had to change my way of thinking, whether I had to change my way of interacting with them to get them to create more ease in their lives. However, with time, I had moved out of that equation in my life. My life was more about the children and their needs, and what I decided were my needs were to contribute to their present and to their future, to create funds for their education. And yeah, I had a need to create my future too... So, if you notice, I came in as an afterthought.

As I commenced with my journey to find myself, I found greater ease with my body, with my emotions. I reduced my tendency to judge my body for what was going right and for what was not going on right. This started to provide more ease with what I could create in my life. I began to create my life, my business with more fun.

I was willing to laugh at myself for any goof ups I made in life, or in business or with my children. This willingness to laugh at myself has moved me away from taking myself and my work too seriously. My relationships with people started to transform to one of greater ease.

Today I connect more easily with people. There had been periods in my life, when I wished to keep away from people and at those times I used to think something was wrong with me. Nowadays if those thoughts should come up, I just don't make me wrong for that. I allow such thoughts to dissolve over time. This "non-judgmental mode" has taken me to a space where I have more ease with myself and again with what I can create and greater ease with what I am choosing to not create.

Step 4: Creating ease with nature

In the past few years, I have let go of a lot of clutter in my body and from my head. I mention body and head separately here as that was the way I used to think of my body earlier. Within a few months of running Access body processes regularly on my body, my discomfort with my body eased. And the continuous non-stop strings of thoughts in my head, eased to a place of fewer thoughts. I have finally begun to get to a place where I can have ease throughout my body — head included!

On most days, I have such few thoughts that I feel like I am in a meditative state without doing any meditation. It's a blissful state. As I work with my clients, I am one with the Earth, the sky and with birds and animals. I notice an eagle soar high and glide across the clouds. Parrots flock around a tree nearby. In seasons where a nearby tree sheds its leaves, I see the parrots conversing excitedly. In other seasons, the green parrots merge with the green leaves. I then see them more often when they move their beaks and tails. Two squirrels play on the roof and make some noise as one squirrel chases another. An occasional butterfly comes by. I am in total gratitude of being alive in my body. These are times when I am totally one with me, one with the Earth, one with the universe. I am grateful of having fewer thoughts that day. The coconut tree whispers to me that its fruits are ready to be plucked. Within 2 days a man who can climb coconut trees miraculously appears and we have coconuts at home! The gifts of nature are plenty. Just watching the clouds glide by is bliss. I enjoy all seasons now. When it rains mildly, my heart sings. When it pours heavily, I start to laugh with nature. I still have a mild difficulty during hot summers. What can I unlearn here to be more at ease with nature?

> With the de-cluttering of thoughts, my awareness has increased. The way I am present to my world and the worlds of people has stepped up. In my current profession in the areas of Transformation and Healing, I am in a position to contribute to declutter, and destress of other people's challenges. And I consider this as a tiny drop of awareness created for that person and I wonder if a ripple of greater consciousness could now get created across the world through this person to more people as this person is more willing to receive more of ease.

On one particular day, a few years ago, two people called me. Both had a back ache, the clearing questions that came up were different. In one case, I asked the caller — where are you expecting support and decided you are not receiving it? For him it was his father, he said. His father was asking him to shift out of his house and wanted him to live on his own. As we chatted, and the clearings continued for a few more minutes, he felt better as the pain had eased.

After a few hours, another person called up. He said he had a back pain that seemed more like a sprain. I asked him "What have you decided is twisted about your office?" The question just popped out of my mouth! He explained that he worked in a company that created gaming software for gambling dens. He had a lot of guilt that, by working in this company he was playing a part in breaking up the homes and finances of people and their families. Clearing the underlying emotional issue began to ease his pain.

In a third situation, I was once conducting a workshop on clearing money issues at a hotel in New Delhi. One participant was in so much of pain, she couldn't sit. She lay down for several minutes at a time, on the carpeted floor as the back ache was intense. After clearing money issues verbally for a couple of hours, for all participants, the lady started to sit up with ease. In her case, some insecurity about money plus fear of having less money in the future, had created the backache.

Our thoughts and emotions create trauma as well as peace for us. The examples above are to illustrate the ways we create trauma for ourselves and for our bodies. There is always a choice in front of us. When I get upset, I look at what would I like to choose. I ask myself 'Deepa, would you like to choose peace or trauma/anger/upset? Just asking that question takes me to greater consciousness... I notice that I have more than the single choice of getting upset. Frequently asking question releases all my charged-up emotions and upset from that situation and I am fine. Sometimes I find that I am not willing to give up the upset in those few minutes. I have learnt to be "patient" with me for such situations too. What if I didn't have to judge me? What if I didn't have to make me wrong? With passage of minutes, hours I give up whatever got me angry. In one rare case it took me 8 months to let go of something! Well, it was still better than the years I was taking earlier and still not letting go!

What if we could heal the Earth though greater communion within our self, creating greater communion between us and people and thus contributing to greater peace in the world? What if we could heal the Earth while willing to be peaceful within ourselves?

What ripple would you like to create, that would heal the Earth beyond your wildest imagination?

> *"And if you are really happy, you may wish to let your face know. Just saying!" – Dr Dain Heer. Co-Creator, Access Consciousness*

The Author

Deepa Ramaraj

www.HealingEarthBook.com/deepa-ramaraj

CHAPTER 8

Crystal Healing Magic

Lezlee Willems

I'm not sure when it was that I first heard about Crystals. I somehow knew something about it even though I had never seen one that I remembered. I remembered lots of things from other lifetimes and it was hard to put into words what I knew. I grew up on a farm on the western edge of Kansas and didn't have friends other than my brothers — until about 5th grade. That's when my aunt, who was my teacher at the time, finally figured out I needed glasses.

With glasses I could start to see other people's faces. Not being able to see kept me close to the ground — connected with the Earth and less distracted with all the nonsense of emotion. I looked down a lot. The Earth kept me whole.

I made things out of natural stuff from the windbreak. The windbreak was a couple of rows of old and mostly dead trees that had been planted at the edge of the farm to slow the winds and snow from whipping around the homestead. This place away from thoughts brought me joy.

There were dead branches so old that they were silky soft and smooth. I so enjoyed tracing my fingers along them and feeling the textures on my fingertips. I was fascinated watching the little ants and bugs climbing all around keeping so busy. The bright green fresh sprouting wild grasses delighted me as late afternoon light shone through them making them glow like magic. Finding bird skulls and making forts out of dead wood was so much fun. Dolls didn't interest me, I wanted to try to catch the ground squirrels, play with the wild kitty cats, or drawpictures ofladybugs, horses and plains indigenous people.

I gathered pretty stones from the quarter mile dirt road that connected my house to the main gravel covered county road. My pockets were always full of rocks. It brought me comfort to put my hands in my pockets and touch them. I played with them quietly for hours in my bedroom.

In about 1975 the craze of gluing googley eyes onto rocks and making pets out of them got pretty big. I didn't understand why they wanted to glue plastic eyes to something that already had a personality. The plastic eyes covered up something that was already there.

I wished for a long time that I could find or make an arrowhead. Then my grandfather found the most gorgeous red and purple jasper arrowhead in one of the fields he was plowing with the tractor.

Mom was so kind to me and drove me all around to where she knew that someone had found an arrowhead. My brother was equally excited about going to look for more arrowheads. I found one almost immediately! Mine was the same color as the dirt. This was before I got eyeglasses though. It didn't occur to me until much later that the stone showed me where it was, so I could find it.

It was explained to us arrowheads were made by chipping off part of the stone. So, then my brother started throwing the rocks onto the concrete walkway to break them apart and see what was inside of them. I was very upset with this destruction. I had a point of view about this and it stuck me. It didn't bother him. He didn't care. He was just having fun. It was light for him. I made the significance of past life stuff heavy for me. I didn't get that the Earth is constantly making new stones. The sense of what he was doing was not honoring the stone and it was not making an arrowhead. I didn't understand it.

He could not feel what I felt when he shattered them. I could not find a voice to express how devastated it made me feel. I just shut down and judged him. Feelings weigh you down.

I played the victim and ran to my room and hid there for long periods many days after. I cleared the bottom of my closet out, set my lamp up in there and hid with my rocks and some cool sparkling beads my grandmother had given me. Finally, at one point I remember packing a handkerchief with a sandwich and tying it to a stick to put over my shoulder like in some cartoon and telling my brother goodbye. That would be great punishment for him breaking those rocks. He ran after me crying and saying he was sorry. If I was conscious, if I was aware, I would never have been that mean to him. The stones were happy to gift that to him. *Where have you judged the Earth is being misused that it was actually happy to gift?*

When I was eleven, Shirley Maclaine was a guest on the Johnny Carson Show and it was past my bedtime, but I ran out of my bedroom to stand close to the TV, so I could try and see/hear what she was saying. She was talking about Chakras and Crystals, and that they had energy. I don't remember much more than that, as my dad was irritated and finally yelled out that she was a stupid blankety-blank.

I loved my dad and didn't want to disappoint him, so I shrank to fit his reality. I quickly shut off my curiosity about Crystals and turned to art instead which was a satisfying and a creative outlet that I wouldn't get judged for much. I could create the same internal space with staring at a blank sheet of white paper as I could while staring at my rocks. *When did you shut off your awareness so that you could fit in?*

After that I tried to do everything right. I became an overachiever. I finally got glasses which made me look smart, made a few friends, went to middle school, won a 4-H State Leadership Award in high school, got a boyfriend, lost a boyfriend, got great grades and earned a scholarship to go to college for Graphic Design.

Fast forward through the wild college parties and the need to have a boyfriend from California so that I had a good excuse to move where

I knew I wanted to go anyway. That relationship ended up in a Jerry Springer-worthy-six-fiancées-pitted-against-each-other sort of trauma and drama. I got a much more supportive boyfriend once I dodged that bullet, and we had many good years but were never married.

But everything I had done during those younger years to shut off my awareness coupled with my amazing ability to lie to myself pretending I didn't know about energy had already shut down my body. I found out later what an amazing gift being aware is and that the heavy stuff I was feeling was *never mine to begin with.* Many Conscious teachers are now saying this.

I had been aware of all the angry and bitter feelings that people have "out there" but thought it was mine because it felt so intense and real. I had turned my awareness in on myself so dynamically that this energy stuck in my face and heart area, creating chronic sinus infections, bronchitis and pneumonia. I had stabbing pain in my head constantly for 12 years, and no allergy medicine worked well enough to do anything but keep me from dying totally. I developed a huge tolerance for pain.

After two surgeries and the doctor telling me one too many times, "You'll just have to live with it," I got mad and finally got responsible for my own health. I didn't know what I was looking for, but a book fell off the shelf at my feet and I picked out a couple more. I changed everything I could think of and turned toward intestinal cleansing and energetic healing of many modalities.

I learned a modality where I pulled Earth Energy up in swirling vortexes through my body and out my hands and the energy of the universe in through my head and down into the earth. Spinning and Expanding and Harmonizing, pulling energy through the torus. It turned on something in me, like turning a light switch on, and I sensed an energy flow of magnitude in my sinuses. It was like laser beams when I put my hands on my face, liquefying all those crystallized feelings I had used to shut off my awareness. I dropped to my knees and gave thanks that I had finally found something that could help people. *It was truly a miracle!* Three short months later I was off all medications and haven't been back to the doctor since. That was over thirteen years ago!

I was almost dying but still more interested in helping all the stupid unaware people "out there" rather than becoming totally aware myself so that I wouldn't have to choose what doesn't work for me anymore.

Up until then, I was sure the world would be a better place if everyone just died. I never even had kids because I didn't want to be responsible for bringing into this world one more body that would have to use resources and overpopulate Earth. I had been destroying the Earth and my body with judgment. I didn't get that *Your Body Is Earth – it is your connection as an Infinite Being to what will Create Greater on this sweet planet, if you connect to her.* Like I did when I was a kid.

I started buying stones to help me heal my body. I thought about how wrong my mom and dad might think buying rocks was and didn't tell them for years, because you could take a walk and find rocks anywhere. Wouldn't they think I was wasting my money? I put that thought to the side and chose to do it anyway because these beauties were what I had always been hoping to find as I filled my pockets back on the farm.

I went to a gem faire wondering what I would learn. I heard there were going to be speakers and one was going to talk about finding dinosaur fossils and meteors. Almost as soon as I got out of my car and started toward the exhibit hall my body started vibrating. If I had not already played with some Healing Energy I might have been freaked out, but I knew that I was in for a treat. All the stones were talking to me at once! I wandered around buying a little of this and a little of that. Yum, better than candy and lasts longer!

I stopped at one tent and picked up a couple dirty looking crystals that everyone was ignoring, and my body lit up even more. They were huge and together only cost me $30. When I showed some other people, they said that each one should be worth at least $70 each. They must have been hiding where I would find them! One is a Citrine Scepter with a couple thick gold rutilations in it.

Then finally I went inside another exhibit hall and I stood next to a giant iron meteor. I put my hands on it for at least half an hour. I was in love. My whole body vibrated with life, and I didn't care what people thought of me standing there glued to it.

I bought a tiny piece of Moldovite from that vendor. Moldovite has a vibration to it that is strong. They say that even if you usually don't feel energy, if you hold Moldovite you will sense something. After wearing it for short lengths of time I became comfortable with it and wear it for days at a time when it suits me. Some people don't sense it at all and others tell me that they can't hug me when I'm wearing it. You wouldn't want to be potent enough to be attuned to something that would shake up the world and make things different!

Crystals have so much to share. Their patterns and colors and complexity, their polished surface that you can see down into like a captured galaxy transports me easily beyond any problem. Some are rough, gnarly and cracked or pitted with the wisdom of the ages. Some are super ugly to look at but make my body feel good anyway. They are doing something with me, the being, and they are doing something with my body, and we are doing something with them. This is communion with no definitions... only possibility.

I get present with my body when I have a stone in my hand. You have to drop your barriers, expand and be present to hear what they are sharing with you. They communicate in energy, not words. You can get to the space where you can be a translator, but the moment you put meaning on it and tell people that _____ is what this crystal does, you limit what they can offer. *What jobs have you assigned crystals to that if you didn't, they could be even more than what you have defined them as?*

I found people to do Reiki with, and one of the ladies had a big crystal that she said was dead. It didn't have any energy. She told me she had buried it in the soil for months at a time, let it sit in a flowing stream, put it in the full moon light, out in the sun, let it sit in a bin of grain, gave it a salt bath. She had done all kinds of crazy things to clear it.

I thought "why would you need to clear a stone?" That is not my point of view! The stones and crystals of this planet are more conscious than we are. They are willing to contribute everything to us and we just take and judge. We need to be willing to contribute back to them, which is what she was trying to do, but she wasn't including her body in the equation.

If other people have touched a stone it is probably from appreciation and enjoyment, so you would need to clear that off for what reason?

She handed me the stone and asked me if I could do anything with it to bring it back to life. I thought it was magnificent! Quartz, but not clear at all, it had all kinds of other stuff included in layers and crusted up on the outside of it. I put all my finger tips on it and connected to the earth to find the place that it had come from and I simply thought, "restore, restore, restore..." over and over until its energy came on. This seemed so natural to me I didn't even think about how I was doing it. Then she said, "ok it's yours." I was thrilled for a moment, then I got the energy "wait a second, that's not what it wants. It wants to stay here with you."

You can charge your Crystals this way too. It's easy and a great excuse to play with them. Then you don't have to cart boxes full of them outside to sit under the full moon, while worrying about whether someone's going to come steal them before you wake up.

Crystals *know you*, they will choose who they would like to own. The question is... will you receive? If you have an ounce of receiving in you, you probably have Crystals in your house. If you don't yet, you are not lost. Let them teach you how to receive! Adorning your body with gorgeous beautiful things is very nurturing and shows the universe that you are willing to have more.

Before I became cognitively aware of my communication skills with the stones, I soaked some pretty things in salt water and ruined their finish — all because some expert told me I should. Please be nice to your stones, if they are pretty and shine for you, is there anything wrong with that? If they are dusty, maybe a rinse would be fine. I have a toothbrush just for Crystals!

Crystals are not tainted from people touching them. I am certain they can be under appreciated just like you have been or done to your body. However, Consciousness includes everything and judges nothing. * And when you BE the Consciousness, you will always override and dissipate any ill intentions.

What you can do

Ill intentions and all that stuff is mental shenanigans of **P**rojections, **E**xpectations, **S**eparations, **J**udgments and **R**ejections. Everywhere that the Earth — bodies, homes, property, soil, plants, animals, birds, crystals, air, fire, smoke and mirrors — have had **PESJRs*** (sounds like Pez-Jr.) placed on them, will you now destroy and uncreate that energy and set them all free please? It's just a choice. People unconsciously choose to do this stuff a lot. Please consciously clear this every day! Simply say "**Destroy and Uncreate the PESJRs worldwide.**" Choosing this would be a huge contribution to healing this planet. This is a tool from Access Consciousness®*

As I stepped more and more into my own power and started constantly looking for what was next for me, I explored the channeling world. I hung out at all kinds of Expos and Conferences and still do to some degree. Now it's just for the fun of it, and less because it is so significant, and purpose ridden. These beings that deliver messages to humanity through a medium or channel don't wish for you to think of yourself as less than they are. You're just different.

---

* Access Consciousness is a grand and ever-expanding toolbox that empowers you to know that you know, co-founded by Gary Douglas and Dr. Dain Heer. I am grateful beyond words to these two magnificent, intensely kind and nurturing men. They teach you to ask questions to generate awareness, not to get an answer. <u>www.accessconsciousness.com</u>

I was online for webinars every week at weird times of the night because the person who channeled whatever angel or being it was, lived in various parts of the world or was online in the afternoon here in the United States. It was a great creation on my part to be self-employed, as that gave me the freedom to override my negative thinking with constantly listening to something that was fun for me while I worked. I changed completely. I even removed the TV from my house and it felt so much lighter. *It was like a burden had been lifted off my house!*

Egypt Adventure

My boyfriend of two decades left when I decided to travel to Egypt with a group of these crazy channeling people who I had never met in person. That was his point of view not mine. I sensed that I had known these people for lifetimes and that I finally fit in somewhere. That online thing freaked him out, talking about energy freaked him out, and he wanted me to go back to who I used to be. I said, "so you liked me sick and angry?"

Never go back, never give up, just keep going. There is something you know is possible for this sweet Earth if you just keep taking any step you know to take, even if you don't understand it. You have to Walk On.

I knew I had to go to Egypt. I didn't know how I was going, but I was going. I cashed in my Roth IRA, and I considered it to be an investment in me. The beings of light I had been working with assured me that I wasn't going to retire anyway so it would be fine. I thought about that and realized it was true. I'm doing what I love, and I would stop doing that for what reason — to lay on a couch and decay? No thanks!

There were a lot of people from all across the world who wanted to go, but could not for financial reasons. We had an online bulletin board system that was clunky compared to what is available now. People were congratulating me and wishing me well, and I wanted to take them all with me. I came up with a brilliant plan that would allow them to participate in a deeper way than listening to our recorded channeled messages after the fact. I offered for them all to get a crystal and record into it what they would like to contribute to the changes we were about to create through this trip.

We were going to be, or at least ask for and conduct, the energy that would break the domination of the "illuminati matrix," just that little thing. It would allow the young people to have a say in what gets created on this planet and override dictatorships worldwide. We went to Egypt near the end of March and stayed a few days after Easter of 2010. Just a few months after that, the revolutions started and became known as the Arab Spring.

I took about 20 crystals with me from people who mailed them to me ahead of time, and early in my adventure I hid them in the wall at the Temple of Queen Hatchepsut. It was important it be at a Goddess Energy place, and what I didn't know until later is that the ground is too hard, and I wouldn't have been able to bury them much of anywhere else that would make the difference we needed it to.

I know that the archeologists will eventually find where I put them, but what needed to happen has already occurred. Hopefully the experts will be perplexed and wonder why they have not found caches of crystals like this in other places. That's fun for me!

Other people who went with me on that trip put their personal crystals in the pit underneath the Great Pyramid. That is not a place the general public ever gets to see. We had a special invitation that was gifted to us by the guardians with machine guns who opened a special gate for us. Some of these beings with bodies are very in tune with what energies can be allowed into a place that is so precious. They don't let just anyone go in there. This was not planned or scheduled by anyone but the Great Beings of Light.

Another Crystal I took on this adventure is a very special one that my mom gave to me. Backtracking just a little, my mom came across a bunch of Crystals in a shop in Kansas and had to get them. She found out that they had been purchased from an abandoned storage locker in Richmond, California in the Bay Area. They had made their way half way across the country and now are back in California with me.

Mom knew I needed to have this one in particular. It is a smoky pyramid shaped, multilayered phantom, filled with inclusions of one sort or another, plus a whole lot of magnificence embedded under its surface. Its shape and faces are in an Isis configuration I was told later by a lady who has a famous crystal shop in Mount Shasta, California.

When I played with it the first time, the room became clear and the floor dropped out from under me. It was like this reality overlapped with infinite possibilities. I was sitting on the floor AND floating in outer space with stars and nebulas, and I could see it with my eyes open!

I call this Crystal "the Activator." I had it with me when I lay inside the Activation Chamber in the King's Chamber of the Giza Pyramid. People call it a Sarcophagus, but no one was ever buried there. It is a place where energy pools and is then distributed along ley lines which are currents of energy similar to meridians in the human body.

I was one of the last people from our group to get in the pink granite box and receive what was there for me. As the others from the group got in and got out, time seemed short to me. Others perceived that people were taking too long and that we might get caught doing this thing no one else is allowed to do. Then it was my turn and I laid down. Time disappeared. I was only allowed 30 seconds, and someone was watching the clock, yet it seemed at least 15 minutes had passed for me.

There were lots of stories from lots of people about what they were drawn to do and how they restored these ley lines. I went on a few of these adventures. There were many groups that traveled the world doing this work. This was a massive effort and we had a lot of "celestial help."

These ley lines have now been restored, Consciousness can never be hidden away again. It is making things very difficult for those who wish to use perversion of power against others for control. Have you noticed the dark squirming? So many of you reading this are the ones who have asked for this, you better pat yourself on the back and acknowledge it so that Consciousness can continue to grow!

During my Egypt Adventure I gathered at least 10 pounds of rocks that I hoped I would be able to take home with me. The dunes are made of sand that is small almost perfectly round Calcite. If you go to the dunes, make sure you get down in that sand and be with it. It is a phenomenal healing! It's silky smooth. You can sense stuff draining off of you. If you have not touched Calcite, please find some and you will get a sense of what being surrounded by seas of smooth Calcite would do for your body. I found quite a few nice sized pieces of Calcite from there that I have yet to make pendants out of, but keep an eye out for that.

I realize now that I have been embellishing the story and saying it was 25 pounds of rocks not the 10 I just compared it to my 10-pound dumbbell! Yep, probably the same. I don't own a scale.

In any case what you are about to read next is awesome! You think things are made up of matter and that it weighs a certain amount. I was only allowed 24 pounds baggage on the flights within Egypt, so I had to pack light. I weighed my bag on a scale I borrowed, and I was just at 23 pounds going into Egypt. When I made the flight inside Egypt with all those rocks added, I was sure I was going to have to pay extra. No, everything together weighed exactly 24 pounds. Somehow 10 pounds of rocks became one pound.

Evidently my stuff chose to contribute to me getting these things back home. The Earth, the rocks, the electronic scale, the Great Beings of Light, perhaps I myself created the bag weighing less. In any case, it wouldn't have happened if I hadn't asked for it. What are we capable of that we are not acknowledging and actualizing? If you acknowledge *what you have created* that was out of the box, more could show up.

I know some of these experiences might seem significant, yet it was never really like that to me. It's just what I chose at the time. I was following what felt light to me to do. This is something that Access

Consciousness finally gave me words to express but what I had been doing all my life. Even when things were not so great, I was always able to get it to change eventually by choosing what was lighter for me.

*There are some things you just know you have to do. You can't **not** choose it. The truth is that you came here to be the change that is required! Yet you think you aren't already doing that. That's the lie.*

If we don't change something, humanity won't have but 20 years left on this planet. The planet will be fine after we go, we just won't be around to enjoy her beauty anymore. I want you to know I'm doing everything in my power to make sure there are people enjoying themselves and what can be created here indefinitely. This information about restoring our communion with Earth is that important. And you can be part of it!

The main thing to create that is to find joy, laugh, relax and stop judging. If crystals aren't where you find this for yourself, please go... do... be... what turns you on! It is time to truly live, thrive beyond surviving. Sustainability is not about just scraping by, and squeezing yourself down to make elbow room for up to 10 billion others. As long as 10 billion others are choosing from Conscious Awareness, that sustainability is possible. It is about creating and generating a future that is continually growing and expanding with possibilities! *For everyone.*

What do you desire to create? Are you going to let anyone, or anything stop you? What if you could choose a level of kindness for you and this planet, you have never been willing to be before? What can you choose that would increase your personal allowance of your Conscious Awareness? What would it take to step out of the judgment of you and everything going on in the world? Would you rather be right than free? Hopefully you got spaced out with all those questions!

Crystalline Light Body

This has been made so significant that it sticks you. No one really knows what this means. Let's demystify this, pretty please!

To *Crystallize* something means to bring it into a solid form — water crystallizes into snowflakes or ice, a structure that is beautiful and pure, minerals crystallize under pressure and heat to form gemstones. The body we've been walking around in is Crystallized Judgment. *Get rid of the Judgment and you will have Crystalline Light Body.* It is really that simple.

Everyone wants to make this significant, hard to do, or worry about never being able to interact with loved ones because you will become some airy-fairy immortal being that no one can see or touch.

Really? Do you *really* want to worry about that? Right now, how many people see you, acknowledge you and touch you with kindness? How often do you walk down the sidewalk and you *would* smile at someone and wish them good day, but they won't even look at you? Hopefully you don't think that you are wrong because no one looks at you. As far as understanding you, do *you* get you?

Who you think you are is a glob of definitions at best. Definition, alone, is a limitation of the infinite energy space and consciousness that you truly be! And it is a judgment that it cannot also be other things. *To define something, is to judge that it Is Not Infinite.*

Totally getting rid of judgment takes diligence. People will judge you when you don't judge. You will pay for the lightness you be by being willing to receive judgment.

I'll give you a concrete example. What is heavy for you is a lie. It is not fun. I briefly dated this guy and we stopped at Burger King to order some fast food. It wouldn't have been my first choice, but it worked to my advantage. Since I had never ordered there before I was unfamiliar with their list of limitations. Ha-ha, I'm being a little funny here on purpose.

I ordered what popped out at me which I was happy with, and then relayed to the employee what my date wanted. Except my date was on the phone and wasn't paying attention to what the employee confirmed as our order. We got the order exactly as I had put it in, and my date said that everything was wrong about his order and that the guy should be fired because he wasn't listening and blah, blah, blah.

This was fun for me but not for him. I was like "oh, this is what judgment looks like, interesting." He was like, "I'm right, he's wrong, you're wrong, everyone is wrong."

I was just watching it and I was aware that everything my date was accusing the employee of was exactly what he had just done. I allowed him to rant while I simply received and pulled energy through him, through me and out the other side.

When we got to where we were going, the tirade had continued and began to escalate because I was not reacting, and he had probably never experienced that before. He was pushing for my opinion of the whole thing. I said, "well, he gave us what I ordered but you didn't correct me when I put the order in." Then he blew up *at me*, instead of complaining about how the employee should be fired.

Even more, I received rather than pushing away from him, I pulled the energy he threw at me and it felt good. I enjoyed it. What is light for you is true for you. You can receive any energy. Judgment is just energy. This was the first time I had put the Access Consciousness®* tools into work in a real-time situation. I was so empowered. He broke up with me soon after.

If you think this Crystalline Light Body thing is spiritual and that means you shouldn't have to pay for it, how is it going to happen? Are you wishing and hoping and praying? If you were willing to invest in what brings your body joy and ease, and not invest in pushing away for protection, would something else be possible with your body?

Choose anything that is light, expansive, ease and joy. Is it a Crystal necklace, is it orgasmic tasting food or maybe champagne, is it a massage? Is it some energetic body work to unlock what you have stored lifetime after lifetime hoping some day you would be able to heal it or understand it and figure all those incomprehensible feelings out?

Whether you call it ascension, or Crystalline Light Body, Christed Body, Mutation, or Evolution – you know something else is possible with your body. The closest thing I have found that will start to unlock these capacities you have with your body are with the Access

Consciousness® Body Processes.* What would it take to have your body be a phenomenal, indefinite, fun place to be?

Bodies need money, you the being don't need money. Did you buy the lie that if you just drop your body and get off the planet that this would create more? Are you trying to figure out what you are doing wrong that if you didn't do it wrong you could fix what it is that is sticking you here on the planet? Or that this is a prison planet? What does that even mean? *The only prison is Judgment.*

You're not here because you're stuck, you're here because you knew you can make a difference! But so many don't want it to be different and they project at you that if you are that wild, if you are that different, it would be bad. Don't buy the lie that you have to get out of here for anything good to happen. If you're not willing to invest in it, it will wait, and you can walk around in the Judgment Suit some more lifetimes. There are more healing modalities than ever before, and they will all work because it is *You the Being Choosing to Change Something.*

There will always be more money — you didn't waste your money — not once. There will always be another job unless you decide you hate work, then your body will shut down too because it likes to work really well. It likes movement, even when you are sleeping. Little molecules and cells spin around and around, just like a galaxy never stops working unless its orbit decays into something else.

For stuff, ask for layaway if necessary. Most merchants who have anything of value would be willing to make a deal for you to pay something off over time while they hold it for you. There will always be another trip, if you missed one this time. There will always be another teacher, and if you can't find a teacher for what you are looking for, *are you it?*

Consciousness, ascension, a new way of being with your body has been hidden but are you going to have it *now* or just hope that it falls in your lap someday? Are you following a lot of experts, or are you going to be the dominant entity in your life? You don't have to look for an ascended master or angel to do it for you. Be proactive. You've got to be willing to take the lead even if no one follows you. You are part of the Universe just as much as any Ascended Master.

Please, ask for what you desire to show up with ease! You may think ascension is just going to happen to you, that you're going along for the ride and everyone will ascend. Yeah, maybe eventually, but are you willing to wait another 26,000 years or whatever it is, for the next cycle? Get over the wait (sounds like weight and that is a heavy lie) and create! What would it take to choose Consciousness now? And now. And now...

The Earth Is a Gem

The Earth is not a grain of sand in the universe — the Earth is a gem! You are not a grain of sand, swallowed up by the masses of other grains of sand on a shore that no one visits.

There's nothing wrong with the Earth. People have been creating so much separation and unconsciousness here that they think we are the only planet with life on it. They think that we are alone in the universe that that even if there are other planets that support life they are too far away to be of any assistance. They have decided we need assistance and can't do it ourselves. Or worse yet, that aliens are coming to get you and eat you. Oh. My. God. Please give that up!

All eyes are on Earth. When I was a little girl I looked up at the night sky and though I couldn't see very well down here on Earth, I could see the stars. Dad was excited about teaching me the constellations and bought a telescope. He made his own stand and tracking gears for it!

One night after everyone else went into the house, and it was just me and the expanses, I thought, "I wonder if there is anyone out there?" and in response, all the hairs on my body stood up and I had a flush of energy run through my body that was powerful.

I shrank. Oh, how I wished that I hadn't shrank from it. They are here to help. They aren't going away, and they aren't landing because how many people on this planet would shrink just like I did? When we can finally open up and receive they will consider communicating a different way, not that this is necessary.

The Earth is finally changing like it always wanted to. There are now more than 10,000 people on her surface being a Walking Meditation, Totally Conscious, Judging Nothing. I still catch myself, but it's getting better all the time.

For over 2,000 years, The Mother has held still, trying to keep from changing to please the point of view that humans have had that you shouldn't change. That if anything changes, then it is all downhill from here. They have decided that Armageddon was the only way out of here and they've tried desperately to bring to fruition a point of view of how it has to be. They think that fighting is what is right.

What if we didn't fight what is going on with the planet? What if the planet isn't dying? What if The Mother is choosing to move forward with the possibilities whether we go along with her or not? Are you going? I am. Whatever it takes.

I know this is not wishful thinking. Knowing is not something that you have to prove. I know I didn't have to come into a body again. There are several channelers who have been mentioning that several ascended masters are finally coming back into embodiment. You can believe it or not, I don't care. For what reason would I miss out on what is happening now, when we've waited so long for Consciousness to be the dominant force on this planet? This is not a destructive force, it is a power to change anything with ease if we allow it. Allowing is key.

You Are a Double Terminated Laser Wand

Quartz does a number of things. It transmits, transforms, focuses and amplifies, and holds an electrical charge, which would be why it can store information. What information are you storing that you don't need to be transmitting? Every thought you have is one you picked up somewhere else. Broadcast Possibilities instead!

Quartz Laser Wands have been used by crystal healers in a variety of ways. You carefully can point it toward the body to cut through the energy body to extract what shouldn't be there. You can stitch the same cut back up as if the crystal is a needle with light thread. You can point it away from the body and suction out a pressure or problem. You can more softly channel energy into a wound and seal it. You can get the energy to flow up and down through the body opening the crown and flowing energy down into the Earth. And so much more! If you can come up with it, Quartz Laser is willing to transmit that assistance in a very precise and targeted way.

There is nothing wrong with the Earth. We have plenty of assistance if you are willing to be the messenger or the transmitter of all that would like to contribute to creating more on this sweet planet. This possibility has never existed before. Earth is a precious gem and everyone in the universe has contributed species here. Let's just say that they have invested in this and care about what happens.

Even the beings who could not get their bodies to work on this planet found a way to tag along for the ride. Unfortunately, many of them didn't like what they got themselves into and that created havoc for our bodies. Now those grids are off the planet and they have been leaving in droves to go back to their expansive "eternities" without the limitation of time and matter. Don't be afraid of them, be kind and invite them to go. Let them know the grids that held them here are gone, that they are not trapped here any longer. Transmit that information. Give them permission to go.

What you can do

You can be a double terminated Laser Wand. Raise your hands to the sky and ask for all the energies that you *can* contribute to the Earth to come, come, come. You will sense your hands start to conduct these energies. Open up and receive. It is time for the separation to end. Open the energy centers in your feet and grow tendrils of light down into the Earth, which will nourish her and your body. Restore your Communion with Earth! Pull, pull, pull, all the energies you *can* contribute to the Earth and flow it down *through* you and direct this light, this information, this energy, this consciousness *through* your body and down into the Earth. Your body has way more capacities than you've been willing to acknowledge. Your body is of the Earth. This will never be more than you can transmit. What CAN you transmit — WILL you?

The Author

Lezlee Willems
www.HealingEarthBook.com/lezlee-willems

CHAPTER 9

Healing the Earth

Gabrielle Lugo

> *"You cannot get through a single day without having an impact on the world around you. What you do makes a difference, and you have to decide what kind of difference you want to make."* – Jane Goodall

Like most children outside was my favorite place to be. I didn't care if I was raking earthy autumn leaves, exploring the tiny magical forest behind my house, or being chased on my bike by the neighborhood bully. I loved the freedom I felt bursting out of the kitchen door, the invitation of the land who was just waiting to play, and the excitement of what I might find around the corner. "Gabrielle, dinner!" my mom would call to me each night as the sun set signaling the end of whatever adventure I was on. I never made it home on time. It was always hard for me to leave my nurturing friend, the land, she always listened to me and seemed to make everything better just by sitting upon her. I had a favorite spot that I would go to each night where I would say my prayers or speak my fears, hopes and dreams. It was like my little nest in the earth. It was here that I felt held and listened to and that anything was possible. By the time I was twelve we had moved twice, far away from my nest, and far away from the child who adored her land. I became someone who didn't fit in and I shut off my awareness to a lot of things, including my connection to my beautiful earth. I wouldn't find it again for a long time.

Over a decade ago I embarked on a journey that would forever change my life. This journey began what I will refer to as my adult awakening, where I recovered and rediscovered my connection to the earth. I learned how much the health of all inhabitants of earth, is vitally important to the health of earth herself. I came to realize that we are all moving parts of one big organism. If a part of that organism is sick it will affect the entire being. I was sick, and I was affecting my piece of the organism. The earth had been calling to me for a long time and I had ignored it. It manifested in my body as anxiety-that-could-not-be-ignored. I had choices, I could continue to ignore it and figure out how to suppress the anxiety, or listen to my knowing and go on a journey. I opted for the journey.

My Journey

It was January 2008 and life was pretty good. I had a great job, a roof over my head and was fairly healthy. I was living life as I thought it should be lived. Seemingly out of nowhere, I was crippled by the inability to breathe. My airway became tight, my breathing shallow and an invisible, crushing weight appeared on my chest. Very quickly, it took over my life; it was in my every thought, and it ruled my day. Anxiety fueled by panic, and I was helpless to the power it had over me. The world I knew slowly fell away. It was as if I was in a well falling deeper and deeper, manically trying to climb out, reaching for anyone or anything to help me, while watching the light slowly fade until I was engulfed in the darkness.

A month went by and I was in the fog of desperation. I felt like nothing could help me and nothing was going to get me through this. I felt alone and scared. My only light in all of this was praying. I prayed to the Universe, the Great Spirit, God, asking, pleading for help. Nothing like this had ever happened to me before and I was at a loss. I wallowed in the fog for another month.

Then one night I was awakened by a suffocating feeling coming over my body. I launched into full panic mode. I tried breathing deeply but the tightness in my chest was too much for any breath to get through. I tried putting my body in different positions hoping that somehow it would help. It didn't. In that moment I broke down, I completely surrendered to whatever was going to happen, and in that moment, something shifted. My body assumed a sitting position and my head was thrown back. Bubbles of energy were being released from my chest and coming up my throat and out of my mouth. I had no idea what was happening and when it was over I fell asleep.

I woke the next morning, symptoms in full flare but I had clarity and somehow, I knew what to do. I needed a shaman, and I needed one close to where I grew up. In hindsight the land that I had loved as a child was calling to me, it had something for me and it was urgent that I receive it now. However, in that moment all I wanted was to breathe again, I wasn't aware that something bigger was happening. As synchronicities tend to happen I found a shaman woman in a town very close to where I grew up. A town that I knew I had frequented as a child.

I phoned the shaman woman and explained everything to her. She agreed to see me as soon as her schedule allowed which was about a week away. I was hoping for sooner and expressed my concern. She was empathetic to me and invited me to begin comforting my inner child and that if I needed to reach out between now and my session to do so. I thanked her and hung up. Immediately I entered the healing energy of what was unfolding; the earth, the shaman and my being were all contributing to my healing.

What follows are excerpts from my journal entries over the few days I took to travel to the shaman and the healing that took place with the earth before I had my actual healing session.

March 19, 2008

I am here at Niobrara State Park. It's Saturday around 8:15 PM. I do believe that I am the only soul – human that is – at this park or at least that's how it feels. When I rented this cabin, they said it was the only one available, yet I see no other cars. Strange.

Many things have brought me here to this space, in the condition that I am in. I know I am on the verge of releasing something that I have been carrying for a long time, since birth, and this is what is driving me. I am so tired and so tired of not being able to breathe but I have to keep going.

I arrived here this morning around 11:30 AM and it was so windy! It's not too cold for it being March but the wind makes it feel cold. During my initial drive through of the park I stopped at a little area with a small lake and a picnic table. Here I was gifted with the feathers of a crow (I think). I found them by the picnic table. Apparently, I was only gifted some of what I gathered because as I stood there holding them a big gust of wind blew all but three out of my hand. Crow is about personal transformation among other things. I guess he and the earth are wishing me well on my journey. I thanked them both, the crow for the feathers and the earth for holding them until I got there. I was tired so back to the cabin we go!

When I got back to the cabin I took a nap and had an awesome dream. I dreamt that an old grey-haired wizardly type of gentlemen came to me and my younger self and told me that this healing that is coming is important and not to worry. I think he was speaking more to my inner child than me. He gave us a stone and told us that if we get scared to hold it and think of him.

Funny thing is, it looks like a stone that I brought for my fire ceremony. He left, and an elderly native woman appeared. She touched my arm and I saw my toddler self in a field. She was in a playpen made by nature, just as happy as she could be. The elderly native woman picked toddler me up and placed her in my lap. After she did this, the native woman turned young. She assured me that everything was going to be ok and they were all there to support me. I could feel the land and its spirits so strongly after this dream.

I set my intentions for my healing session, and said many prayers during my fire ceremony. I feel very held and protected by this land and her nature spirits. I am all alone, yet I feel very loved and cared for.

March 20, 2008

I'm here in Madison and tomorrow is my session. I'm so excited to talk with someone about this and I hope she can help me.

Last night after my fire ceremony I was exhausted, so I went to bed. I was awakened by one of the strongest thunderstorms I've ever heard or seen. Gale force winds, lightening, thunder so loud that it shook the cabin, and rain so heavy with drops so big it sounded like hail, but I think it was just rain. I can't help but wonder what things I shifted during that ceremony and if the earth wasn't helping things along with the storm.

***

Just a bit ago I was so scared because I could not breathe. I felt like I was on the verge and was gagging and shaking. As I sat down to write, thinking that might help I just started to cry because I just can't take this anymore! I called on all my spirit guides, and animal guides to help with this discomfort because it was just awful! They must have heard me because I now feel a little better. I can at least half way breathe. I hope I'll be able to sleep.

***

I pray that I can release this energy tomorrow! I so hope I can. I know I can. With everyone's help I can do it!

March 21, 2008

Before my session I had time to spare so I had decided to visit a place called Devil's Lake State Park. This was a place I thought I had been to as a child and upon entering the park I knew I had been there. I decided to do a short hike.

I am sitting here on a bluff at Devil's Lake. It's so freaking cool I can hardly stand it. What's even better is that somehow, I can breathe. I can breathe and there is barely any heaviness on my chest. This is so wonderful! Thank you, thank you, thank you to this land for holding me right now. As the tears come so does my gratitude.

March 22, 2008

Before I write about my session yesterday I have to write about what happened after my hike. On my way out of Devil's Lake I saw a sign for Steinke Basin. Something was pulling me to go there, and I still had some time left before my session, so I decided to go. As I pulled up the parking lot was pitted with big water holes. I didn't want to risk getting stuck, so I decided to turn around.

As I turned around I looked at the land and I instantly had déjà vu. As I pulled away I kept looking at the land and it kept calling to me. The farther away I got the sicker I felt. I probably got about a mile or so away and I turned back around. This time there was a car in the parking lot, so I knew I wouldn't get stuck. I pulled in and got out. I began hiking the trail but that didn't feel right, so I walked back towards the parking lot. There I found a bench and sat down. As I gazed out at the land I felt so much love come over me. I felt I had been here before.

I closed my eyes to meditate and I knew this is where my toddler self was, this was the land from my dream.

As I talked with my toddler self she was reluctant to come back to me and I really couldn't blame her, she was in paradise. Eventually she did and as I stared out across this land that had been a part of me for so long I opened my heart and thanked the land and the people of the land for taking such good care of me and for keeping me safe. As I did this I was staring out at the tree line and I could see the native people who had cared for me and could feel their love. They walked into the trees and I didn't see them again.

I was in the perfect place, mind and spirit when I got to my session. The session helped me move much of the heaviness out of my body, and being, and when it was over, my breathing was better. Over the next few weeks it would return to normal.

After the Journey

I realized there is no difference between the earth, and God. They are just unique expressions of the same energy, each playing a different role. She answers prayers, and she provides guidance if we just listen. Each time I step outside, go on an adventure or sit quietly in nature, I learn something new about myself. If I am struggling with life, I simply take a walk, invite her energy to come along and the space and nurturing she provides opens a space in me where my knowing shines through.

The land is what called me, invited me to heal myself. The land gave me a firm punch in the arm letting me know something was ready to be shifted, something that I had been asking for only back then I had no navigation tools. She was saying, "I'm ready to help you when you are." When I was ready, I listened, and I followed path so clearly laid out before me. My connection to the earth after this healing was so much stronger, I had found what I lost, and it's made all the difference in my life.

Contributing to the Earth

Not long ago I found myself sitting on a rock above a beautiful mountain lake. I was gifted these words from the earth. "I am dying, the keepers of the land are gone, bring joy back into people's lives, sing the earth's sorrow, sing my voice." We have disregarded the earth as we have evolved. You can see it through extinctions, deforestation, and the pollution in our water. At times I feel completely overwhelmed and wonder how I can affect change and healing for her. Contributing to the earth can be as simple as expressing daily gratitude or lazing on the grass feeling the breeze on your skin and the sun on your face — enjoying what the earth is gifting to you. Everyone finds their own unique way of contributing to the earth. Half the fun is asking — "Hey earth, how can I contribute to you today?" The other half of the fun is receiving her response and creating together. I have found the most profound way for me to contribute to the earth has been by starting from within. By healing myself, I heal the earth. As I heal and become my true self, I invite the stranger's I meet and the people in my life to choose differently, and the ripple affect continues to multiply affecting people I've never even met.

My desire for earth's children is to awaken to new possibilities in our relationship to the earth so that we may co-create a paradise never before seen by time. The earth is truly our mother and she loves us and we as her children must tend and care for her. We cannot survive without her. Now is the time for the new keepers of the earth to come forward. Now is the time to find our joy and live from our hearts. Now is the time for us to speak for the earth and what we know is true. It is time to sing a new song.

What you choose to do in the world makes a difference. What will you choose?

The Author

Gabrielle Lugo

www.HealingEarthBook.com/gabrielle-lugo

CHAPTER 10

Attachments to Truth

Bre Pryse

As an energy healer and a coach, I get asked many different things. Like all others in my professions, I have people come to me with a variety of problems but still seek the same answers: how can I fix this, change this, or make life work for me better?

As much as we would like to believe it is true, there is no one answer that fits everyone. Why? We are unique beings on a unique journey. The more we honor this uniqueness both in ourselves and others, the easier and more fulfilling our lives can be. We can then be able to create what we desire to create instead of just problems to solve. This choice of self-empowerment is imperative at this point in time in our existence.

I, like so many others, believe we are at a crossroads in our evolution and planetary existence. Due to pollution, climate change, resource shortages and a variety of other factors, we are finally waking up to the fact we need change. Big change. Changes in the way we live, Changes in the way we think. Changes in the way we treat our lovely

Mother Earth. We are quickly approaching the point where we have to change or die. Many people might argue we are past that point. I personally don't think so but — it is here soon.

Empowerment is a concept many people struggle with. Since what has been labelled The Great Recession, many people have seen big life changes. Many have realized that there is a need for more empowered choices, creation of new possibilities, and basically shedding the old ways that don't work anymore. As much as we love and are attached to them, many of the old ways of operation don't work anymore. Big changes require big choices and even bigger actions. A total change in attitude if we wish to continue on our earthly journey.

When I am asked "What is the one thing I can do right here, right now that would heal myself and my planet?" I have a bit of a standard answer: Get out of the box. We need new out-of-the-box thinking to make changes we can't even see or fathom right now.

That's a very tall order that has to start with small steps. Small steps allow for us to make missteps, evaluate as we go, and change as we see fit. It also makes it easier to keep the new course and not get distracted. Chances are you know someone who is an out of the universe thinker. The ideas and energies are so beyond this reality that they probably can't be used for generations if ever. Starting out small can help assure that the end result actualizes faster.

Starting is the key. Many suffer from decision paralysis because they don't know how to even begin. There are many modalities and teachings about how to start. Some teach one has to shed negativity before one starts. Some teach that one needs a clear vision. Some teach that beliefs must be aligned. There are teachings that match every philosophy under the sun.

After many years in this business, I have several recommendations. My biggest often takes people by surprise. Ready? *Start shedding attachments to truth being the ultimate power or weapon.* This concept makes many people's heads almost explode. Let me explain.

Let's look at truth. What exactly is it? Believe it or not, many different definitions exist. All that matters is how one personally defines it. So, take a few moments and define what it is. What is truth to you? What isn't it to you? If you have some old thoughts and beliefs about truth that no longer serve you, allow yourself to change them. Create new ones that align with who and what you are now.

We are told from a very early age that truth is the ultimate. Children are often punished for not being in it. I don't know about you, but I have childhood memories of being punished because someone's version of the truth changed without me knowing. Or my version differed from others. These memories do an awful lot to shape our world and our relationship to truth.

Being in someone else's truth often determines how many rewards we receive. It is our way to money, power, God, and a lot of other things. So why would that be bad?

So, what could be wrong with truth? Here are a few things to think about:

1. Truth is often defined as static.

This means there is one truth and only one truth about a situation. Can that be accurate? Look at the many different versions and opinions people have of the same events. Eye witnesses often give varied accounts. One views something through their own experiences, judgments and expectations. This can mean that many different truths exist.

2. Once a "truth" has been determined, other possibilities can become invisible.

Have you ever noticed that once you have the answer, you shut off a lot of energy that has been dedicated to the problem? Got an answer, get on with life. But... is it the highest possible truth? Could there be a truth that is even better? How many times have you had an issue and decided what the resolution was only to have the universal energy forces fix it in a way you never dreamed possible? Most of us have had that experience at one point or another. Wasn't the universe's solution far easier than the one you had decided was "the truth"?

3. Truth can give birth to judgment, self-righteousness, hatred and many other traits of close-mildness

We can become very attached to our version of the truth. It makes us right and the other person wrong. If that wasn't energetically intense enough, it can often become more closed off to other possibilities and other ways of thinking. Currently, we are experiencing people from all aspects of life being ultra-focused on their beliefs/opinions/truths and trying to force them on others. Of course, that is meeting with lots of resistance and anger. Change is needed but many of these are ultra-focused with loads of judgements and no regard for other people's points of view. Do you react to other people's thoughts and opinions? This can be a sign of attachments to your own truths.

4. If truth never changes, that would prevent you from changing.

Personal change needs to happen to enact world change. If we are focused on the one truth of who we are, it can only make change harder. The world changes at a very fast rate. Why wouldn't truths change with it?

If one holds onto truth with a vice grip, it would stand to reason that personal change would be very hard. Have you allowed yourself to change? Are you still the same person you have always been?

I have had a very unique healing journey. I started out working in fast food and absolutely loved it. It was a place where I could shine, and I think I did. I then moved to computers first becoming an operator, then a programmer and a data processing manager. While I enjoyed computers, the stress of being in management made me sick. I chose to work for small companies with lots of problems who were in a fight to survive. It became too much stress and illness set it. The doctors offered me neither help nor positive options, so I decided to explore natural healing aspects. And I chose yoga. Through a variety of happened stances, I learned that I was a natural energy healer.

So, over the next few years I spent learning energy work and how to look at life from a different perspective. As you can imagine, my logical brain and spiritual brain often had problems. Being a programmer where everything must be in a certain order and work a certain way into the spiritual realm where everything is an unknown was quite a journey. A journey that was not always easy, but I have always cherished.

Spending so much time in the corporate world in a position that requires a lot of logic allowed me to create a bunch of skill sets that I can use to help my clients look at issues from a variety of perspectives. Now with over 14 years doing this work, I've attracted a lot of different people with a variety of issues from diverse walks of life. I can honestly say I have seen many things and have learned an extraordinary number of things. One of the biggest: we must always be learning, shifting and changing to create what we chose to create.

More than 14 years have passed, and I'm thrilled that I took the journey. Has it always been easy? No. Do I regret doing it? Never.

Here are some things I have learned that I would love to pass on to you to make your personal journey an easier one:

1. Allow truth to be dynamic. One of my first teachers recommended I start a journal. Great advice. A few years later, I read it and didn't recognize that person at all. I strongly believe that if we are choosing to live to our utmost potential, we should change dynamically. That requires changing the truth of us.

2. Get rid of judgments. We are loaded with them. The more we can get rid of, the more energy we will have for us.

3. Allow others to have their own opinions without you having to change or react to them. We spend a lot of time and energy trying to change people who have no desire to change. Allow them to be who they are and use that energy elsewhere.

4. Choose to have personal change be easier. This isn't an easy real-

ity, but we can ask for it to be easier.

5. Be in a more expanded awareness of what is going on around you. Sometimes we only see what we want to see. Have the courage to choose awareness even when it isn't comfortable.

6. Practice good self-care. Be kind to yourself with your thoughts and feelings. Eat food that is good for you. Replenish water and minerals as the body needs.

7. Allow yourself to consume information without having to turn it into truth. In this world of fake news, modified news, manipulative news, there is very little undistorted news.

8. Be in allowance of change. We can spend a lot of energy trying to stop change. How much energy could you reclaim for you if you stopped blocking change?

9. Get out of the Right or Wrong paradigm. If something is right, the opposite may be wrong. What if instead you chose empowering vs. disempowering? Is this an empowered choice? Will this empower the future I desire to create if I chose it?

There are many other things, but these are top on the list. These are very tall orders that can take time and energy, even one can go a long way to create a new and more empowered you.

When we change ourselves, we change the energy of the earth. The denseness of our judgements and disempowered choices really weigh the energy of the Earth down. The more we can clean up our energy, the more energy the Earth has.

More importantly: the more awareness we have, the more we are able come up with inspired solutions to even the most unfixable problems. Wouldn't it be a lot of fun to help change the planet for the better just by being a true version of you?

May your journey with truth be a fabulously productive and profitable one!

The Author

Bre Pryse

www.HealingEarthBook.com/bre-pryse

CHAPTER 11

The Gift of The Golden Sun

Rebecca Trodden

Oh, the Glorious Sunshine...

Did you just see a sun rising in your mind after reading that? Did it tweak the memory of the sand and the ocean from a holiday you've taken? Did you sense the joy of the feel on your skin from it? Our skin THE biggest organ our sweet bodies have. Ahhhh.

How many time have you been out side and looked around and took noticed the lushness from the trees, the grass, the blueness of the water? However, when is the last time you gave gratitude for the gift of the Sun?

How many times has the sun been noticed when its presence is not there?

Or when the sun finally comes out in the spring, the warmth that permeates your being from the inside out?

I remember as young child the gift of a sunny day and playing outside doing one of the many things kids do, riding my bike to the store while enjoying the heat with the ride. I remember the long hours of gardening and enjoying the sun warming my back. Playing in the water barrels at grandma's while the sun was a blazing. Naked. Oh, the laughter and joy. The gift of childhood summers at grandmas. Play.

I've been gardening for the past few years now and love overlooking the garden and asking for the sun to embrace and bring my garden the sweet sunshine to create and nurture the soon to be ripe veggies. I so enjoy biting into a fresh picked carrot and washed from the ground. Or the juices from a peach from a farmer's market. Mmmmm. Mouth water. I've often found myself talking to the plants or to the fairies in the garden and having full conversations with them. How many times has the openness of speaking freely during those moment have I heard a little tip or trick or learn of some magic to bring more life to the area.

Have you planted anything. You put this tiny seed into the black dirt. Down beneath where the sun doesn't even shine. Burry it where only warmth is noticed until its time. And what time? Only that little seed knows just when that golden perfect moment to open, from the inside and break free from the safety of the shell and wiggle its way up thru the dirt to the warm sunshine above. Only to burst free into the sunshine and awaken to the light above. Its stretches its core and keeps growing.

How about the fairies in the forest? With the sun streaming in little slivers thru the trees. Oh, do enjoy the trees, climbing and looking at the faces in them. When was the last time you took a walk in nature, marveled at the trees and the earthly smells? When was the last time you listened to the silence and yet the rhythm of the earth? The fun can be at any age, by anyone. Shall we only choose it. Have you ever sat by a babbling brook and listened? We were lucky enough to of had a creek on our property as a child and wed go often go tad pole hunting. then little frogs. Smiles abound. maybe find a fresh water shrimp or too. we played with the water and I would often just stop and listen. Maybe the horses were in the pasture also and they'd venture to us and play along.

In nature, you become one with everything and everything becomes one. What connection do you have to nature you've forgotten or don't take time for? Is it time?

What really does the sun contribute to us each and every day we've yet over looked? What gift is the sun to you? What would it take for us to embrace and gift the sun the gratitude to it for the receiving we do with it every day. From the food we eat to the animals it cares for, to us and our amazing sweet bodies. To chasing the newly fallen moon. It is in equal terms half of the part of what starts the tide change for the new day to come. How many pictures do we take of it and often stop in joy of the moment when it rises and falls. Ahhh, the golden rays.

My question is what healing capabilities does the sun have that we've yet to fully acknowledge and receive? And what gift is it we are so quick to create a comment out when it's too much or too little for us?

Or how about the gift of it sun setting for the night? Fires, fireworks and campouts, and the twinkling of the stars. Warm fires, friends and wiener roasts and the joy. All the colours dancing in the fires enticing your mind to imagine and play.

Then during winter, oh how I love winter, Okay I was born in it so it's easy for me to love. the feel of the snowflakes landing on my face. Maybe you ski or snowboard or do another winter activity. You wake in the dark bleed hours to hurry to get the fresh powder. During the winter months of shortened sunlight, we rush outside to embrace all it is gifting us and make the most of the play. know of friends and family that have been mimicking the sunshine with the use of these UV lights during the winter. Healing thru the use of them. What would change with our bodies and the earth if we were to receive with the ease the golden rays it so eagerly gifts us each day.

It's often had me wonder if truly is where the main starting point of the nutrients come from to create on the Earth. And how many ways it starts the creations cycle of the as if you watch where no sun shine shines very little will grow. Yet Where there is plenty of it and the warmth it creates vast amount of lushness.

The golden sun has this amazing counter partner the golden irides-cent moon. The many phases it goes thru and with each day can be smaller or larger. Yet never less or never more. Always just what's required. How many times have you stared at the moon and stars and embraced all the night offers. As a child I remember sleeping on the trampoline and looking up with my siblings and laughter. The joy of childhood at enjoyment of the fun of sleeping in sleeping bags and just the moon. We knew the house door was open and safety was only a mere few feet away, and a light on to lead the way. Maybe a mother up still, to kiss the fear away and remind us to get some sleep.

We laughed, told jokes, may if we were lucky had a fire maybe help make it and s'mores before too or maybe we read books and used flashlights to enjoy all the adventure brought to us each new time. We welcomed the fun.

Each time the sun rises its different, each time the moon rises its different. In this moment I truly get the gift in the new in a whole new amazing way. Each day and night bring new gifts and releases the things from the day in amazing ways.

Do we let go of the old and welcome the new, with each passing mo-ment or do we hold to to it all in hopes it never leases in fear that we won't have the joy or fun again?

When your living in the moment it's the moments that count. Not counting the moments that create your true JOY.

What endless adventure can you create with the sun and moon today? Better yet, what joy will they invite you too now?

The Author

Rebecca Trodden
www.HealingEarthBook.com/rebecca-trodden

CHAPTER 12

River Goddess

Trudie Jane Lorna Crooks

I'm MOTHER EARTH....

From the depths of my deep earthy waters that flow calm and vigorously through the heart of my soul!

I wonder are you listening?

My heart beats like yours an even bigger beat to sustain all 7 billion people that I support!

I'm fully ALIVE and CONSCIOUS and communicating to you!

Be still in this present moment now and receive the gift I'm sharing it is not to be dismissed in anyway.

As my waters flow throughout the Earth from the rivers to the lakes and the oceans, I have never stopped flowing and nourishing your bodies being the breath of life for you in every moment.

I'm running out of patience and tolerance with mankind you can experience it through my intense natural weather from volcanoes to tornadoes to hurricanes to floods to fires to temperature extremes.

I'm letting you know shifts and changes are now required in humans on my beautiful planet.

This direct message is to wake you up and have you become a Steward of the Earth!

I'm RIVER GODDESS...

I'm calling in Spirit, GOD, Universe, Source, Divine, Mother Earth, Angles, Fairies, Guides, My Team, my mother, everyone and everything to contribute to this message for Healing the Earth!

I have been given this assignment to be a faithful steward of the Earth.

I'm so honored to be chosen.

The beauty she expresses and shows me daily through her magical magnificent waters continues to capture the very core of my being, my heart, my soul.

I'm standing up to express the healing of Mother Earth through the flow of her waters it becomes so crystal clear.

What a GIFT she is to me!

What a GIFT she is to each and every being on this planet.

Are you now ready to be the GIFT back to her?

It all starts with you being a Steward of the Earth!

You ask, "What is a steward of the Earth?"

It's simple!

To be responsible, take care of and look after it

Mother Earth!

Are you willing to BE the GIFT to her?

NOW is the time to increase CONSCIOUSNESS, ACKNOWL-EDGE, CONNECT, CONTRIBUTE and NURTURE her!

BE in the JOY OF LIVING on her beautiful planet!

CONSCIOUSNESS

IS AWARENESS THAT INCLUDES EVERYTHING WITHOUT ANY JUDGEMENT OF IT!

Be still in this moment and get aware of Mother Earth, everything you know about her.

Let that awareness flow through you with no judgement!

This is CONSCIOUSNESS keep receiving more and more information.

Anywhere that you were blocking or stopping or limiting your awareness let go and let it come flooding in like her waters.

Many people are unconscious here on planet Earth and it's time for an awakening to become conscious stewards of the Earth.

Ask questions about the Earth to increase your consciousness and be willing to receive the information that will help you become a steward of the Earth!

When you ask the question, do not come to conclusions looking for answers, just ask and follow your awareness when it comes to you, so all the possibilities can show up!

ASK and RECEIVE is the biggest law of the Universe!

Ask the Earth what she is requiring for healing?

I wonder what her perspective is?

Keep asking the Earth!

Remember she communicates!

Be still, go in nature and listen to her.

Are you open and willing to be conscious here on the planet?

If so, do whatever is takes to choose that path to heal yourself and Mother Earth!

Earth healing is going to require mankind being conscious here on this planet and choosing your own healing too.

That is a choice you can make right now.

It's time to be conscious, raise our vibrations and abilities to bring forth changes that will heal the Earth and all beings on it.

Since I have chosen to be conscious and be on my healing journey here, I have been given this opportunity to bring forth this beautiful message!

I wonder what may transpire in your world when you fully choose to increase your consciousness and begin your healing journey.

You may be the one to heal the Earth!

ACKNOWLEDGE

accept or admit the existence or truth of
recognize the fact or importance or quality of
express or display gratitude for or appreciation of
accept the validity or legitimacy of
show that one has noticed or recognized (someone) by making a gesture or greeting
confirm (receipt of something)

Acknowledge the GIFT she is to you right now, she is the oxygen you breathe, she is the water you drink and cleanse in, she is the food you eat, she is the ground you walk on, she is everything to you!

If it wasn't for Mother Earth, you would not exist here on this planet.

If she didn't provide life you would not have life!

Most of mankind is using and abusing her in so many ways whether its unconscious or conscious it's been happening for generations.

We can all start choosing to change this behavior!

No more tolerating ABUSE with each other and on Mother Earth.

It starts with each and every person acknowledging and becoming more aware of what is so and choosing differently.

Time to wake up my friends to how lucky we are to be here on her planet.

Shifts and changes are required, and the time is now she is letting us know!

Just like the weather is shifting and changing here on planet earth, do not underestimate her forces that can shake us all of her planet if she desires.

Mother Earth is so graciously nurturing 7 billion people on the planet.

Can you imagine the impact if 7 billion people started waking up being conscious, acknowledging, connecting, contributing and nurturing her!

That is a possibility starting with you, one person becoming aware of what she is requiring.

I'm so grateful for Mother Earth and I'm willing to acknowledge her everyday going forward being a Steward of her Earth!

CONNECT

bring together or into contact so that a real or notional link is established
join together so as to provide access and communication
associate or relate in some respect
think of being linked or related
provide or have a link or relationship with (someone or something)
form a relationship or feel an affinity

Be connected to Mother Earth, go out in nature, go for a walk or a hike be outside, and you will find her all around you.

Take your socks and shoes off step onto her earthy ground and feel that connection you have with her.

She as a message for you there!

Are you willing to Connect with Mother Earth?

She is awaiting that moment with you specifically.

As I sit on a beautiful rock in the middle of the River to connect with her, water is flowing all around me from the left to the right and underneath me.

The beauty I'm surrounded in captures my heart and soul. The water, the trees, the leaves, the rocks, the ground, the birds, the fish, the blue sky, the wind all that I perceive.

I'm in pure JOY of the Earth and her waters she is a magnificent delight to connect too.

I connect with every sound, every drop every splash, every movement, as she flows through me reaching every cell and molecule of my being.

As the river continues to flow my water starts flowing too and I come into full communion with the Earth.

I perceive that I'm ONE with her experiencing flow, calmness, peace, freedom, joy, beauty.

I'm so grateful to be here at this time on her Earth.

There is no difference between me and the River.

No difference between me and the Earth.

We are not separate we truly are ONENESS in totality.

We are all connected and ONE with Mother Earth and Each Other!

CONTRIBUTE

give something in order to help achieve or provide something
help to cause or bring about
supply for publication
give one's views in a discussion

CONTRIBUTION

a gift
the part played by a person or thing in bringing about a result or helping something to advance

Mother Earth's Contribution to each of us happens in every breathe, every moment, every movement you experience!

How can you contribute and BE a contribution to Mother Earth?

Keep asking questions and more questions it will create more awareness and possibilities to come through.

I wonder...

What did you come here to contribute to her?

What contribution is she requiring from you for healing?

Do you have something to give back to the Earth?

Can you speak something forth for Earth healing with your voice?

What healing can you bring forward?

She is NOW ready for your contribution!

Contribution is about who you Be here on her planet!

Remember this is about being the Gift she is to you!

Her beauty takes my breathe away with the joy of living, and I journey into her deeper message!

Deep, deep, deep in the depths of her soul messages continuing to arise from her flowing waters to wake up the deepest parts of my soul.

What would it take for mankind to flow with these energies on my planet?

NURTURING, CARING and KINDNESS

Theses energies could change the entire planet!

It starts with you being willing to live that way.

You may have many questions on how to Contribute and be a Contribution!

Contribution is "a GIFT"

What Gift do you have if you would start being it would heal Mother Earth?

Be the Gift you truly are and step into your greatness for Earth Healing!

Are you willing to wake up and be your gift, talents, superpowers, magic that you truly be?

You can start being a contribution right now in this moment. Take time to connect with her, talk to her remember she is alive, breathing, and listening to you.

Communication and Connection is key here.

Ask her questions and listen to her whispers.

I'M A STEWARD OF THE EARTH...

Mother Earth I choose to be conscious of you, I acknowledge you, I'm connected to you!
I will contribute and be a contribution to you!
Mother Earth I will nurture you the rest of my days here on your magnificent planet!

NURTURE

care for and encourage the growth or development of
help or encourage the development of
cherish (a hope, belief, or ambition)
the process of caring for and encouraging the growth or development of someone or something
upbringing, education, and environment, contrasted with inborn characteristics as an influence on or determinant of personality

Thank you for receiving this message from Mother Earth and River Goddess!

Grateful

The Author

Trudie Jane Lorna Crooks

www.HealingEarthBook.com/trudie-jane-lorna-crooks

CHAPTER 13

What on Earth, Does This Have To Do with That?

Eena Basur

When I was 11, my mother, beautifully and patiently with diagrams and drawings, explained to me, what menstruation is, why it occurs in female bodies. Of how it's an egg that forms every month in the womb, that then, if I choose to have babies, can be fertilised by a man's sperm, if not it would simply bleed out every month. These are not her exact words, but what I summarised for myself.

Shortly after, I had my first period — menstruation, chumming, that time of the month — commonly referred to as, '*I got down*'. It was an intensity that I had never experienced before in my body, and, from this point onwards, came to know and refer to as pain, severe pain. It was literally getting down for me.

I was an athlete, a runner and tom-boyish. And, for some reason, I decided, that menstruation is the suffering that was brought upon women. That me being a woman was a curse, and that I couldn't run, I couldn't be an athlete, I couldn't do all that was fun for me, when

I was chumming. That, it was something that required to be hidden and kept secret from men. That it's going to be painful. And! Was I true to my word!? I created all of that and more. That time of the month was like, as if joy has been sucked out of my life.

It's funny to me now, that I would associate something that gives birth, that is the source of creation, as suffering and pain, rather than fun and ease. Was it true or just a point of view that I had bought as real and so solid, that it took years for me to get to a point of choosing to change it and allowing something different to show up?

I used to abuse my vagina, swear at it and ask for my uterus to be removed... every month while chumming, even after being married to a gorgeous gentleman who absolutely brought my body alive. Up until, I found the tools of Access Consciousness.

For the first time, I was willing to see the beauty of having a woman's body and the gift that it can be to create a different possibility, a different future, rather than using it to bring me down and keep me there. My fight with and for it, was keeping me locked up, jailed, stuck, by nobody else, but me.

To think that I am not the creator of my life is a lie so disempowering. To know that I am, allows me to create beyond. If it was my choice to pervert my power against me and my body, then, it was my choice to change it, when it was not working. The pity, the sympathy, the empathy that came with it, had started to show itself for what it truly was — an obligation to stay limited. It had to go, change, shift. Something else had to show up now.

So, I started to talk to my body, which I hadn't really truly done before. I was willing to be weird now, if that is what it took to change it.

Alongside this conflict and war that I had going within me, there was a similar one going at a much larger scale, in the country.

When I was in school, all the way up till when I was in first year college, women were being burnt alive in India. The town that I lived in and the neighbouring states of Punjab, had it high, in numbers.

There was this insane sense of anger for, with and towards women and their bodies. And, even though the source of it seemed men, I suspect, that wasn't entirely true. In India — the land of the Kamasutra — oddly, sexualness and pleasure with your body are denied and suppressed at an epidemic level and was peaking in those times. Then, there was religion and politics that were targeted to win at any cost. I wonder, if it was all of that, and more, and something else. I don't have total clarity on the secret agendas at play, however, I do know, it was an interesting time to be a girl around then, when it was being projected at you, that you are someone who could easily be raped, abused or burnt at any point. The lies of safety and security seemed to be raging rampant and being abused a natural outcome.

Women were being burnt alive on their wedding night, and girls at birth, often times by other women with the justification of being a burden to them, to the world, to the planet — for they won't be able to provide for themselves or others.

There were different people responding differently to this — there were supporters, there were the accusers, there were silencers, there were the rebels, there were the reactors, the actors, and other variations, and, then there was my family and extensions — the activists.

My family of activists — raised our voice. We raised it to bring light to the on-goings in the world. We did it through community theatre, where a group of us would come together, talk about it, become present with what our points of views are about it, sometimes awareness, sometimes judgements, and put together a play that we would then travel with to spread a different message, a different possibility.

At the time when women were being burnt alive, we created a play, that was called, 'Main jala di jaungi' — 'I will be burnt alive' — a satirical take, the funny side of the reasons for burning women. We performed over 150 shows all over the city we lived in, and those of adjoining states, including villages and small towns. By the end of 150 shows, it surely became way more hilarious than it was to begin with. At times, we couldn't keep ourselves from giggling, even while delivering a serious act of the play. The director, my uncle, would try lining us up to get us to be serious, but couldn't keep himself from grinning, giving away what we all were now experiencing. It had started to create a lightness in our worlds, and in the world. Seeing the funny side of things, can lightly, softly, gently invite a different possibility into being.

The thing with fighting for a cause, though, is that it requires you to make that, that is not true, as real, first. We do that pretty much with everything in this world of problems being issued to us on a daily basis, where we have got to take a stand for or against. Because if we don't, we don't care enough, we are spineless, we are not committed, may be even heartless, we are not smart or intelligent enough or supportive.

Somewhere during all of this, I had bought into the whole trauma and drama attached to being a woman, being a girl, in this world and that I was required to take a stand, this way or that. I would argue and debate with women and men, alike, more so with myself, to create these connection points and mostly, to fit in, somewhere, that were not creating something different, only maintaining the status quo.

And, what does any of this have to do with the Earth?

Is it true that women are a burden on the Earth? I know that's not true.

And, if that is not true, who or what am I fighting?

I was putting myself up against a lie, and playing my part in making it true, and then putting on a complete gear with guards on, to fight it. In all of that, where was I?

When I chose to change it for me and my body, one of the key awarenesses that I received, one that surprised me quite a bit, was the underlying point of view that I was resisting, I was also creating as true for me — of being a burden on Earth.

It reflects and creeps up, even today — in conversations, in business, with creations, in my relationships, with my body, and as me. Some of the initial symptoms were, wanting to finish a sentence rather quickly, being apologetic of taking up space, mostly having a sense of being wrong. At other times, I would be fighting it trying to prove me right. Quite a conflict. Not much freedom of choice.

How much of what's going with the Earth — let's say, conflict — is a reflection of what I am choosing? Is it possible that I can choose to be what I would like to create?

To turn around the sense of being a burden, to something greater, I started to ask the Earth everyday, "What will you like to receive from me today," and to flow to it whatever it required energetically. I also practiced increasing my receiving by asking the Earth, what it would like to contribute to me that day. This simple ask every day, has been a much bigger gift than I can perceive in its entirety.

I am learning so much about me from the Earth. Choosing to ac-knowledge that I am a contribution to the Earth has started to change it tremendously for me, to begin with no pains, no cramps and total choice with periods. I started to ask my body and the earth to contrib-ute to what I was creating. It started with the simple choice of ease with making me active and generative even during my periods. My body started to get periods before or after my travels, making it easy for me to create around the world, while enjoying my body and ador-ing it. That started to reflect in all other areas of my life and being.

The thing that I have learnt about me the most from the Earth is, that I am ever changing, so is my life, so is my body, so is the world, so is the Earth, if I let it.

Is Going Green enough?

For a moment, if we were to say, there are no plastics on the Earth any more, no pesticides, no landfills, only natural ways of disposing waste, solar panels and natural ways to generate clean energy, and water is abundant. There is also hate, judgement, anger, wrongness, guilt, shame, regret, lack, polarity. Will the planet thrive?

It is so valuable for us to have a look at what are we choosing and what are they fueling? Are they creating more of what we don't want to create or what we will like to and can create?

Sometimes, it's just about becoming present with it enough, for a door to a different possibility to open. And, the most important, is for us to realise that we can be and are the key to that door.

The conflict within started to change and continues to do so - when I stop fighting for or against and start looking at what I desire to create.

A bunch of people created it, with their points of views and spread it around freely. Now, if that construct doesn't work anymore, what could I create, what could we create and be that is different, that makes that irrelevant.

The Author

Eena Basur
www.HealingEarthBook.com/eena-basur

CHAPTER 14

Walking with the Earth

Cassie Hepburn

As a child I always had a fascination and a connection with the earth and nature. It was where I would go to escape the conflict in my family and the bullying at the private girl's school I attended.

Down the hill from my home was an area called The Flats. It was a solitary child's oasis. The sides of the road were flanked by ditches filled with frogs and water skaters and tadpoles in the spring. There was a number of horse stables and many people who kept horses on their property. Hanging out with the horses created so much joy in my world.

At the end of the road was the slough and the Fraser River. There was a path that ran along the banks of the river and when the tide was out you could explore along the sand and clay banks. The air was fresh, fresher than at our house up the hill with the busy road running out to the university.

I would often see herons, kingfishers and other water birds and in the morning the air would be filled with birdsong. This was also a riding trail, so sometimes I might meet a horse and rider and on precious rare occasions, I was the rider.

Every spring an entire pasture was filled with daffodils of every kind and shade of yellow and peach. A leap across the ditch, between the slats in the fence and weaving beneath the apple trees I would gather the daffodils to take an armful home to my Mom. There was a sense of wholeness I experienced in my exploration of the Flats. I felt most at home in my body and on the planet when I was in nature.

As I grew up, my retreating to nature to seek my wholeness continued, despite being very much a city girl. In high school in the late 60's and early 70's I became aware of the environmental movement.

I lived in Vancouver, birthplace of Greenpeace. It was kind of a natural step. My best friend and I marched for peace and the environment.

In grade nine, Paul Spong, who worked with Whale research along the BC coast came and spoke at our school. I was awed by what I heard that night. His close encounters with the whales, how he played his flute to them and they responded and how the orcas led him back to shore one night when a sudden storm came up and he was out in his kayak. At that time whaling was still quite active on the planet and many species of whales were endangered and at risk as populations were dwindling. I rejoiced with other schoolmates when widescale whaling was abandoned.

I wrote letters and made phone calls and for a time in my early 20's worked part time with the West Coast Preservation Society, their primary focus was stopping the culling of wolves throughout the province. Wolves being culled so that people could sport hunt for moose and deer made no sense to me.

I also assisted Insight Expeditions with a media event and promotions. Their vision was taking business people on a heritage yacht to Haida Gwai where Haida elders took them into the forest, to the natural hot springs, the point being to reconnect them to the land. One of the partners in the venture was Thom Henley who worked with the Haida First Nations to stop the logging of South Moresby Island.

By the mid-80's I began working with children again as a preschool teacher. I loved taking the kids into the forest, any place in nature and exploring what we could discover together.

The desire to be part of healing with the earth grew even more after reading a Times article and seeing what Sting was doing in the Amazon rainforest. I reached out to him and he was interested, as were a number of other musicians in being part of a concert I was organizing for the environment in Vancouver. Sting was working with indigenous people in the Amazon at that time. And then as everything was falling into place I stepped into a relationship, quickly became pregnant, and allowed it all to slide away when my son died.

That was the catalyst to dive deeply into healing myself. I began going to the sweat lodge studying healing, reiki, shamanism and learning about essential oils. Nature and the earth were always there woven through all the healing. The place I returned to always for wholeness.

When I chose to move out of the city to the country that love of being in nature created such a space of healing.

I was in a relationship now with a man who also loved being outdoors and we spent a lot of time on the river, hiking and exploring. We lived on a horse farm and it was amazing to waken to the sound of horses whinnying outside the window. Or the coyotes howling on their nightly hunt.

Always my place of comfort was nature. Sitting on the earth, watching the flowing waters, the flight of the birds, the changing seasons.

I began to pay attention to messages, the owls, the hawks, the eagles. The winged ones would come with messages of encouragement and often come in the oddest places to make sure I was paying attention.

My relationship with the earth and her creatures continued to deepen.

I became more aware of how there were certain places my body would relax and melt in the environment I was in. I would become part of everything, the mountains, the lakes, the trees, the creatures that inhabited those spaces. A glimpse for a moment into that space of oneness, I had always yearned for.

Several years ago, I came across the tools of Access Consciousness and the capacities I have with the earth have continued to grow and expand from sensing waves of delicious blissful energies that move from the earth, the trees, the mountains, the sea, through my feet into my entire body.

Every cell and molecule is alive and the sensation sometime goes on for hours.

Earth Healing to me is about how we walk upon this beautiful planet of ours. Do we walk with gratitude and wonder? Do we take the time to reach into the earth and marvel at all that goes on beneath our feet? Are we in awe of the power of her volcanic core, the crystal caverns, the layers of rocks and underground caves and rivers?

Did you know there are communication networks of trees beneath the forest floor, the fungi mycelium networks that share nutrients and information amongst plants that may be vast distances apart?

I have moved from fighting for the environment, and the earth into looking for what I can do and be to be the change I wish to see in the world.

Some questions we can ask ourselves:

- Are we mindful when in nature?

- Do we make sure we leave our picnic and camping spots more pristine than when we arrived?

- Are we caretakers of the earth? Or are we in fight or resistance to those who may seem out of step with what is required on the earth at this time?

- What would it create if we were to live in harmony with her? Do we choose to be joyful and kind rather than angry and seething with hatred?

- What if you and I can be the antithesis to what is being perpetrated in our world and upon the earth?

- What if each footstep, each moment we walk aware of the wonder all around us, the gift that the earth and nature is to our bodies and being, what if that counteracts every act of terror done upon her?

- What if our joy, our sense of appreciation and adventure is the greatest healing we can bring to our planet?

- And what if it is not us doing a healing TO her but rather a mutual gifting and receiving between us until we reestablish our bodies to be in constant communion with our precious planet? The way our bodies were designed to be.

I am starting to realize the more I am my true self, the more of a gift that is to heal the Planet. My laughter, my Joy, brings more healing than all the protest marches I walked in.

Yes, I will always still choose to take action and speak out when necessary and if what the Earth requires to shake off the hatred and violence and stupid choices that mankind is making right now, is my Joy and laughter and willingness to gift to her, I will make sure that is part of my daily practice.

The Author

Cassie Hepburn

www.HealingEarthBook.com/cassie-hepburn

CHAPTER 15

She Whispers Softly... Are you Listening?

Tanya Desaulniers

Oh Mother, I adore you. I am so grateful for your love and your infinite supply and for the honor of your presence in my life, every day.

The Earth is our Great Mother and I have heard her whispers and guidance since I was a very little girl.

She is more like us and more like our bodies than we can even fathom.

For example: What we call "meridians" in our bodies, she calls her "lay lines." Within our bodies we have the ability to send energy from one part of our body to the other through these meridians and this keeps the energy balanced and flowing throughout our bodies. This keeps us strong and healthy and vibrant.

She is a Body, in fact, she's the greatest Body of us all and through her lay lines that also run from one end of the planet to the other, she has the capacity to send energy in whatever form is required from one area to another.

Imagine an area of land on the planet where water is depleted and very much required. If she is aware that it will create more to send water to that area, she will do so.

She sends energy and information and whatever is required from one end to the other.

Over time and due to the abuse of many parts of the planet, some of these lay lines have become damaged and even severed so sending from one area to the other has become a challenge for her.

She asks us for our help.

She calls upon her children to "Remember me" and she will show you a multitude of ways in which you can contribute to her.

What can we do?

We are designed to heal with her simultaneously. There are many who are following their own awareness and placing Crystals into the Earth at certain points and know that this is offering her the healing she's asking for.

For me... She asks me to sing to her, to dance upon her Belly, to laugh and love and Heal and remind others of her Infinite Love and presence and while this Is offering that healing energy to her, it also heals me.

Communion is a simultaneous gifting and receiving and Communion with the Earth is like nothing else you will know.

Today I invite you to Remember her. She loves to remind me of a quote from a children's book that I read to all of my daughters when they were little.

"I am your Mother, you are my child. I am your quiet place, you are my wild."

I invite you to tap into her infinite Love and chat with her, sing with her, dance with her in communion.

Call upon her if you have ever felt lacking in your life of thatwarm Mother energy. Perhaps your own Mother was unable to be what you required? Call upon her and she will comfort you. Perhaps you, yourself are a Mother? Call upon her for strength and Wisdom and she will aid you.

Her presence is immense yet gentle. All knowing, yet kind.

She Loves you with an Ancient and unwavering love.

She loves you just as you are.

I invite you now to relax to begin by taking in three deep cleansing breaths, deep into your belly and release.

Allow your body to fully and completely relax. Drop your shoulders, relax all the muscles in your face, continue this breath while you consciously allow each area of your body to fully relax.

Now, imagine a glorious divine light pouring down from the Heavens and washing over you. Washing over your head and over your face and acknowledging that everywhere this light touches you, it also warms you and heals you and allow this light to continue down into your neck and shoulders, and your arms and down every vertebra of your back.

Allow this glorious healing light to flow now into your chest and your heart, pooling in your heart.

Healing your heart.

Allow this light to continue into your tummy, surrounding and offering infinite healing to all of your organs and digestive tract and into your waist and hips and pelvic area.

Allow this light now to flow into your thighs and hips and knees, calves, ankles and feet.

Allow this light now to flow into the Earth. Deep into the Earth.

Flowing down past the bones of the Ancestors; those who dreamed us into existence and those who are yet to come. Allow this light to flow down into the Crystal and mineral caverns and further down through the underground streams.

Allow this light now to flow all the way to the very center of the planet. To the Beating Heart of the Great Mother.

Pause in this presence of her and feel her Beating Heart. Feel her infinite and unconditional love. Allow her to surround you and hold you in her Love.

Here she reminds you of her presence in your life. She reminds you that for some, she has been long forgotten and that now is the time to remember her and reconnect with her; to simultaneously gift and receive with her once again.

Bask in this glorious love and allow it now to heal you.

Allow any messages or Wisdom to come.

Just Be here with her.

And when you are ready, allow this glorious light to flow back up.

Up, into your feet, your ankles, your calves, your thighs and waist and tummy and into your Heart. Notice now that you are completely connected, as above, so below and that you are Eternally one with all there is and with your Great Mother.

Allow this light to expand from your heart Centre, 360degrees all the way around you like a great central sun. Expand this infinite light 3 feet around you. 30 feet around you.

300 feet around you. Allow this light to expand out past the home you are in, the town you are in. Past the province or state you are in, past the country you are in. Allow this light now to expand out to

surround the entirety of the Earth and pause here for a moment and acknowledge the infinite oneness you naturally Be with your Mother.

Notice the Love you be with her.

Allow this light of you now, to expand past the Solar system and way out into the Universe. And now expand farther than you've never expanded before. Bask in this space and ask:

"What more can I be and receive with the Earth today?"

"What Communion with the Earth is possible now that has never been possible before"

"What more can I be and receive with my Eternal Mother?"

"What Space of me is possible now that has never been accessed before?"

"What change is possible now that has never been possible before?"

"What would it take to vibrate at this frequency every moment of every day?"

This is the vibrational frequency of the Earth.

"Mother, show me how I can be of the greatest contribution to you and I Thank you for your eternal love and immense presence in my life."

Just Bask in this love and this peace and this space of infinite communion and infinite possibility.

And when you are ready. begin by taking in 3 deep cleansing breathes and becoming fully aware of your Beautiful body once again.

Wiggle your fingers and your toes and stretch out any parts of your body that desire a little more space right now.

Today and each day, you can begin by asking Her.

Mother, what contribution can I be to you today?

She will show you.

Stay in that space of infinite love and communion with her and enjoy a relationship beyond what you've ever known.

She whispers softly... are you listening?

The Author

Tanya Desaulniers

www.HealingEarthBook.com/tanya-desaulniers

CHAPTER 16

Healing Bodies and the Earth with Communion

Julie Oreson Perkins, CLC, ACC, CF, CFMW

In the beginning, there was connection...

I can't remember where or when I first heard this, but it has been intriguing me for a very long time: our physical bodies are composed of the same things as the Earth.

Science's theories talk about the Earth and subsequently all its creatures being created from stardust. When you look at the key elements in both a physical human body and the Earth, there are many in common: oxygen, carbon, hydrogen, nitrogen, calcium, sodium and magnesium, just to name some. A good example of that is water or H_2O (hydrogen and oxygen): Slightly more than two thirds of the Earth's surface is covered with water — and slightly less than two thirds of the physical human body is water.

Plus, there's these interesting concepts:

- Since our bodies came from the Earth, then they will return eventually to it — and to that original "dust" (as in the English Burial Service text of "dust to dust" that was adapted from Biblical text of the book of Genesis.)

- Creation myths — also known as cosmologies (the ordering of cosmos) — of many cultures, traditions or religions also describe a similar starting point that involves "dust" or some other nature feature or creature of the Earth.

Personally, it's fascinating to observe when both science AND religion point out this connection with facts, faith and a variety of documented stories and oral histories. It's an amazing validation of what I have always innately known about our bodies' connection with the Earth — yet wasn't always willing to acknowledge or work with for many years.

... and then there was communion!

Beyond connection is communion. What's that? And how is that different?

One of the definitions of connection is a relationship between things — and in this case of the Earth and a physical body, it's how one causes the other or shares aspects with it. To me, connection is just the starting point — the "hook up" so to speak.

After that, in communion, the connection deepens — becomes much more intimate, honoring, trusting — and allows for the simultaneous gifting and receiving of energy that is completely devoid of judgment and brimming with possibilities. In communion, the energy thrums — or vibrationally hums — and there's an energetic congruency between things.

I'm often asked how that shows up for me...

When I am in communion with the Earth and all things, the visual outlines of objects become more crisp and vibrant — the rest of my physical senses are heightened along with that highly tuned eyesight. Plus my body is so So SO enlivened and full of JOY! My body smiles more — and laughs a whole lot — in that communion. And where and when does that happen the most for me? Walking in nature — camping in the woods — touching the trunk of a tree — swimming in the ocean — being with the energy of what I call "original Earth" in gorgeous outdoor spaces — saying "Yum" to that thrum.

Tapping in: an experiment

As you read that, could you tap in and perceive the natural ease with which this communion occurs? If so, continue to tap in and observe that communion between bodies and the Earth. Stay super curious — like a very observant scientist — and now notice what your own body is experiencing as you continue to tap in...

If you didn't perceive the energy of communion between bodies and Earth while reading, it's OK. Truly. Please don't judge yourself. A lot of people don't perceive it at first. Yet from my perspective, it's easy to begin to commune again with the Earth because of that natural connection — that connection that is as natural as the sun rising and setting every single day.

I invite you to pause here and try this experiment:

- Place your feet on the floor — and focus on your toes.

- Wiggle your toes, like you were wiggling them on a sandy beach of one of the Earth's vast oceans.

- Wiggle those toes more — and again — envisioning the waves washing over them, each time allowing your wiggling to sink them deeper and deeper into the Earth.

- Perceive with all your senses: the various smells of the ocean and its creatures — the sensation of your skin being kissed by the sun — the taste of the salty ocean spray — the view across the many miles of the ocean's surface all the way to the horizon — the sound of the waves gently lapping around your ankles.

- Continue to wiggle — Wiggle — WIGGLE!

- Ask to perceive and receive that communion between your body and the Earth.

- Invite the vibrational hum into your body with each inhale.

- Bask in the thrum of communion between your body and the Earth.

Pause. Reflect. What's going on for you, right now?

Unhooked

Hopefully, you're experiencing the joy and PEACE that comes with communion with Earth — and acknowledging how easy it is to have that?

That's the good news — that it's easy and natural to have and be that... please remember that, as you read on.

The news that we may not be wanting to look at, is that many of us (myself included) have been choosing out of that communion...

Whether we've been conscious of that or not, we have been making choices that "unhook" our connection with the Earth, so that amazing communion is no longer possible.

For what reasons would we choose to unhook? There are many — plus they vary from individual to individual. From what I've noticed, they all stem from "unconsciousness" — from being unaware.

For what reasons would we choose to be unaware? The first time I was asked that question, I was offended. As an adult, I took pride in being intuitive and observant — something that I had invested time, energy and money in over many years. I had participated in all kinds of talk and somatic (body) therapies — life coaching — healing modalities like Reiki, naturopathy and shamanism. I fell in love with the Earth and nature aspects of shamanism, so I began studying extensively around the world to learn more about this nature-based spirituality and ancient healing practice.

So how could I NOT be aware, after all of that — let alone CHOOSE that unawareness?

Healing Bodies

Shamanic techniques, rituals and ceremonies revolve around accessing the healing energy or "medicine" in the spiritual realm and applying it back in this reality to the physical, mental and emotional aspects of the body. As I learned, my connection with the Earth was rekindled and deepened. No matter what tradition I was studying or where I was on the planet, shamanism invited me to become more honoring and trusting of — and more vulnerable with — the Earth and my own body as that extension of the Earth. There was more peace in my world — and my body was more at ease...a welcome change to the dis-ease that I had been experiencing in the forms of breast cancer and severe adrenal fatigue. Without a doubt, my rekindled and deepened connection with the Earth was healing my body. That was one step forward from where I was at the time...

...and then there were two steps back, as the saying goes. I had spent many "intensive" weeks sitting in circles, rattling and drumming, taking copious notes in leather-bound journals. There were do's and don'ts — right ways and wrong ways. It was a quest to "get it right" so that I wouldn't dishonor the traditions or the healers that went before me. I'd go to trainings — practice with colleagues — make miraculous leaps in healing my body — then return home and attempt to recreate that, only to shift into neutral (or reverse!) on all the progress I had made. What was going on?

Enter Access Consciousness®

After finding shamanism and making some healing progress only to have that stall, I wasn't looking to try another healing modality. By this time, I had completed my life coaching certification and had decided that was as good as it was going to get — and that I should be grateful for the progress that I was able to make. I was incorporating shamanism into the life coaching when clients were open to it and things were changing for clients and myself, albeit slower than I knew was possible. One day I was on a healing journey asking for "medicine" for a couple of family members plus more tools to augment the "body" aspect of my Mind, Body and Soul coaching.

And that's when I became aware of Access Consciousness the Bars® — for the second time. The first time I had concluded that it wasn't "right" for me because I had so many points of view about how energy should or shouldn't be managed (and the facilitator of my first Bars®-class definitely didn't do that properly, according to all my shamanic training!) so I rejected it. Yet here came the Bars® again — showing up in a sacred space — and I had learned not to ignore such divine guidance, so I gave it a second look.

With gentle touch to 32 points to the head, a Bars® session releases all the thoughts, feelings, emotions, decisions, beliefs and judgments from any lifetime, that are electrically stored in the brain. With this and other tools of Access, I learned not to assume that there was something "wrong" — or "right" even — and to ask questions to bring up the energy of a situation to look at from an energetic perspective, instead of judging it as right or wrong or good or bad.

Judgment Daze

From Access, I learned what the energy of judgment can create... in a word: limitation. Anytime I was judging something as wrong or bad (also known as negative polarity) — or even right or good (positive polarity) — anything that didn't match that judgment could *not* enter my awareness.

How much of my awareness was being limited by judgment? Megatons. No wonder I was in a bewildered stupor — a daze — unable to really know what was real and true for me and my body!

There I was, learning how to be a healer — and being healed by properly executed techniques — while applying the steps of master healers to build my intuition so that I could really "know" all of this for my-self. Yikes. How much more could I invalidate my infinite awareness? And my body's innate healing capacities?

As I look back on this now, my body is chuckling at all that — and I'm smiling at just how limiting that place that I was functioning from, truly was.

I had bought that shamanism was "the" way — without ever really asking what would work for me and my body... without acknowledging what I knew to be true for us. I'm grateful that I did at least ask for that healing energy and for tools for the body that one day, however — because it opened the door for me to see just how much judgment was running my life.

With that ask, I received — and I shifted from learning how to "do" intuition, to be-ing aware.

Since then, I've been choosing awareness — and consciousness — and asking the Universe and the Earth to "show me" where I am choosing and being unconscious. So that I don't lapse into the unawareness, that disconnects my body from the Earth... and that disavows the Earth's and my innate healing abilities.

Consciousness includes Everything — and Judges Nothing

Grateful for the awareness that I had been judging a lot (and everything, honestly!), I had a new mission: eliminate all judgment. Ironically, the first thing I did was decide that shamanism and its teachings (and certain teachers) were "out of integrity" for how they had "treated" me in certain circles...when all I was doing, from my point of view, was embracing the shamanic principles and making them my own. What a way to "stop judging" — by starting to judge them all back?

Once I stop reacting to that, I started asking this question: what contribution can shamanism be to my life? My living? My coaching practice? My Access business? Having known — truly known — that Earth connection, the healing miracles that are possible and the potency of that, I was reluctant to just pitch all of it. What else was possible here that I hadn't yet imagined?

I asked this again and again — until I really got clear about what they often say in Access: Consciousness includes Everything — and Judges Nothing. That's when I realized that I could "have it all" and create what works for me. What I also was realized is the gift that my being and my body are to the Earth — and what a gift the Earth is to us. For what reason would I refuse that? I chose to keep that — and be in communion, rather than just simply in connection, with the Earth. How does it get any better than that?

Gifting and Receiving

Many people are often able to see and experience the healing nature of the Earth. They know that they feel less burdened after walking the dog, especially if it's along a wooded path or out in an open field or in another favorite nature spot. Yet if asked why that is, I find that many can't explain it — they just "feel better" and are grateful for that.

That's an excellent start — AND I'm inviting you to more by looking through my eyes for a moment, at your favorite spot in nature on this gorgeous planet...

...What do you see? More precisely, what DON'T you see?

I challenge you to find any trace of judgment there. The trees are not looking around comparing their trunks and branches to that of the other trees — the squirrels aren't wondering if their fur makes them "look fat" — the Earth isn't wondering if it's a gift or not.

They all just BE — they all have a consciousness of their own — and they gift and receive without judgment. Aaaahhh... bask in the energy of THAT for a moment.

Kinda makes you want to run outside and lie on the Earth and melt into it, doesn't it?

I think we all get what a gift the Earth is — do you know what a gift you and your body are to it?

Remember: our bodies are of the Earth — extensions of it — which is how they can gift and receive with ease between each other.

Have you considered gifting back to the Earth? Do you realize that the Earth requires energy to shift and change — and that your body may have the energy needed for that, at any given point in time?

Having had a lot of pain and intensity in my body over the years, I've noticed that it dissipates quickly if I:

- Acknowledge (not ignore or override) the pain or intensity

- Thank my body for the awareness of that

- Gift it to the Earth... on the count of 3! And a 1... and a 2... and a 3!!!

This takes care of nearly ALL the intensity in my body. And because I no longer judge energy as "good" or "bad" — only energy that can be available to create, play and change with — I'm able to gift even very "intense" energy to the Earth since I know it will be able to transmute and use it for whatever is required.

Here's a favorite story about that: in October 2017, I went to Costa Rica for the first time to attend an Access Consciousness class there. On the shared shuttle from the airport, I was getting to know my co-passenger and talking about my shamanic training. She was curious about how that relates to using the Access tools, so I described to her much of what I've already told you here: the connection and communion between bodies and Earth — the gifting and receiving that is possible — the absence of judgment in nature. I was happily talking away, when quite suddenly, I felt extremely sick to my stomach — so much so that I asked the driver to pull over and let me out. It was almost midnight — and quite foggy — when I leapt out of the van, expecting to vomit everywhere. Yet the minute my feet hit the ground, I remembered to introduce my energy to the Costa Rican landscape. All I had to do was energetically say, "Hi! It's me, Julie! Just wanted to let you know that I'm here..." and I gifted all that intense nausea energy to that patch of land there by doing a bunch of 1-2-3's!!! Instantly, the nausea vanished. I took another minute to slowly turn and gift more energy in all directions — and my body felt better still. Back in the van, I asked the driver what that place was: he said that we were between two of the famous national forests and volcanoes of Costa Rica. And with that, I knew that my body was the one that could contribute a required energy to that magical space of landscape at that time — and that my willingness to do or be whatever was required, contributed greatly to both the Earth and my body.

I know it can be this way for you too. Next time you experience intensity in your body, I invite you to gift it to the Earth on the count of 3... and receive the instant freedom from it!

(The) Healing Earth

There are hundreds of other stories that I could share that illustrate the healing potency of a communion with Earth. Simply reach out to me and I'll happily share a few over a cup of tea or two!

Until then, I'll leave you with this: the notion that we can heal our bodies AND the Earth, every time we:

- Choose to be aware

- Are Joyful.

- Laugh!

- Acknowledge the healers we innately are.

Will you join me in that?

With oceans of gratitude until we meet somewhere on the gorgeous Earth!

The Author

Julie Oreson Perkins

www.HealingEarthBook.com/julie-oreson-perkins

- The End -